THE ART
OF
BARTENDING

THE ART
OF
BARTENDING

MARK BARRETT

J. W. at Mountain View Downtown
6/21/98

B
BERKLEY BOOKS, NEW YORK

THE ART OF BARTENDING

A Berkley Book / published by arrangement with
the author

PRINTING HISTORY
Berkley edition / November 1997

The Putnam Berkley World Wide Web site address is
http://www.berkley.com

ISBN:0-425-16089-0

PRINTED IN THE UNITED STATES OF AMERICA

10 9 8 7 6 5 4 3 2 1

This book is dedicated to my mother,

ELEANOR BARRETT

This book wouldn't have happened without the work of Jessica Faust, a true professional who must have been an expert surgeon in another life; and Gertrude Bregman, who tells it like it is.

CONTENTS

FOREWORD

A professional bartender, a true doctor of mixology, knows how to make hundreds of different drinks, and he knows every recipe by heart. Knowing these drink recipes inspires confidence. It does a medical doctor's reputation no good, after all, if she refers to a textbook while the patient is in the examining room. The same is true of the mixologist whose customers are bellying up to the bar.

Knowledge of drink recipes is actually a small part of a professional bartender's job, however, and that's where this book comes in. It picks up where all others leave off and gives a step-by-step approach to entering the field, learning the ropes, and polishing your technique until you—yes, *you*—become a truly professional bartender.

Bartenders earn a good income, and they have a lot of fun while they are working. Bartending jobs are available almost anywhere in the world, from big-city nightclubs to country taverns, cruise ships, corner pubs, trains, planes, large hotels, suburban restaurants, bistros, cafés, gay bars, truck stops, strip joints, and tropical resorts. Someday, bartenders will work on space stations, at lunar outposts, and in colonies on distant planets.

If you are new to bartending, use this manual to gain insight into what bartending is really like. It will help you get your foot in the door to an interesting and financially rewarding career. If you are a working bartender already, use this manual to learn a few new drink recipes, jokes, puzzles, and trivial facts with which to impress your customers and co-workers. In other words, blind them with science and baffle them with . . . you know what. It never hurts!

Good luck, and may your tip jar always be overflowing.

ONE

ALL ABOUT LIQUORS

As a professional bartender, you should become intimately familiar with the products you serve. It is a good idea to taste all of the wine and spirits as well as the other ingredients you will be using to mix cocktails. Do not attempt this in one sitting, however, or even in one week; your judgment might become impaired. Do it over a period of time, but be sure to do it. This knowledge will help you make better drinks, possibly create your own cocktail recipes, and answer your customers' questions.

Let's start with the liquors. Liquors are distilled spirits. They may or may not have flavors added, but they are generally not sweetened. All liquors—all alcoholic beverages, for that matter—are required by law to display a proof number on the label. This number indicates the alcohol content of the beverage and is twice the actual percentage of alcohol. In other words, a bottle marked 86 proof contains liquor that is 43 percent alcohol. Bacardi 151, for example, is 75.5 percent alcohol. Homemade grain alcohol, or moonshine, can be as high as 190 proof. Danger! Do not use near open flames! May cause blindness, death, or irresponsible behavior!

Be aware, however, that if you blend two alcoholic beverages together—say, Kahlúa (53 proof) and vodka (80 proof)—you do not end up with a cocktail that is 133 proof, but one that is about 66 proof, depending on the proportions used. In a mixed drink the proof is the average, not the total.

By the way, the alcohol in alcoholic beverages is *ethyl* alcohol. Don't even *think* of mixing up a cocktail using the rubbing alcohol from your medicine cabinet. That stuff is something else entirely and it would probably kill you.

BASIC LIQUORS

Vodka

Vodka is distilled from a base of either grain (corn, barley, rye, or wheat) or potatoes. It is first distilled at over 190 proof and then combined with distilled water to bring the proof down to a level that won't kill you. All vodka is bottled between 80 proof and 110 proof. The final product is odorless, colorless, and tasteless. That's what the manufacturers claim, anyway. What they actually mean is that the alcohol isn't flavored with anything. You won't mistake it for water, but it doesn't have a distinctive smell like bourbon or gin.

Vodka is ideal for cocktails because its neutral character allows the taste of the mixer to come through clearly. Perhaps this is the reason vodka has become the most popular alcoholic beverage in the United States. It has long been the national drink of Russia and Poland, but the Poles and Russians don't mix it with orange juice or tonic water. They chill it and drink it straight up. Flavor is sometimes added by placing a red pepper, a lemon or orange peel, or some other ingredient in the bottle and allowing it to sit for several weeks. There's nothing like an ice-cold shot of 100 proof Russian vodka flavored with hot pepper to get you through a Siberian winter!

Most drinking establishments carry the leading vodka brands: Gordons (U.S.A.), Smirnoff (U.S.A.), Stolichnaya (Russia), Absolut (Sweden), Finlandia (Finland).

Vodka is produced all over world, and there are countless inexpensive "no-name" brands that may be used as the primary pouring vodka, or well vodka. Because all vodkas are similar in character, only a true expert can tell one brand from another, and only when it is served straight. When vodka is mixed with orange juice or tonic water, it is almost impossible to distinguish different brands. Anybody who claims to be able to tell an Absolut and tonic from a Stoli and tonic is full of bull.

Gin

Gin is made from distilled fermented grain (corn, barley, oats, or rye) and flavored primarily with juniper berries. In fact, the word "gin" may be derived from the French word *genièvre*, meaning juniper. Gin can also contain flavoring from dried lemon peel, coriander, cardamom, angelica, caraway, licorice roots, cassis bark, grains of paradise, or various other botanicals. First produced in the Netherlands in the seventeenth century, gin is now manufactured in many countries around the world.

London dry gin is an aged gin which is a pale golden color. Genever gin is a clear Dutch gin that is not aged. Most drinking establishments carry the following brand-name gins: Gordons (U.S.A.), Beefeater (Great Britain), Tanqueray (Great Britain), Bombay (Great Britain), Boodles (Great Britain). There are many no-name brands of gin that may be used as the primary pouring gin.

Unlike vodka, gin has a distinctive taste. Each distillery has its own secret recipe, and taste varies greatly from one brand to the next. Some have compared the consumption of gin to "drinking liquid flowers." Others, myself included, believe that all those exotic ingredients in gin lead to unusually painful hangovers.

Rum

Made from the distilled juice of sugarcane or from distilled molasses, rum is colorless at first, but color is often added by aging it in oak casks or by adding caramel.

Although it is produced all over the world, most rum is still made in the West Indies, where it originated. Light rum comes primarily from Puerto Rico and Cuba. Dark rum comes primarily from Jamaica, Barbados, and Guyana. The most common brand-name rum in the United States is Bacardi, which is made in Puerto Rico. The Bacardi distillery produces three-quarters of the rum consumed in the United States. Other brands include Mount Gay (Barbados), Myers's Dark (Jamaica), Captain Morgan (Puerto Rico), Lemon Hart (Guyana), Cruzan (Virgin Islands), Malibu (Barbados).

Rum has a very strong flavor and mixes well with fruit juice. There is a difference in taste between brands—Malibu, for example, is flavored with coconut—but most of the light rums are indistinguishable from one another. Rum is bottled at not less than 80 proof, and one brand—Bacardi 151—is 151 proof and highly flammable.

Tequila

A clear liquor distilled from the fermented mash of the agave plant grown in Mexico, tequila derives its name from a province in Mexico and is a close relative to the Mexican alcoholic beverage known as mescal.

Tequila has a strong odor and taste and is usually consumed in straight shots. The traditional way to do a shot of Tequila is as follows: lick the back of your hand between the thumb and forefinger; sprinkle salt on the moist area; lick the salt; immediately swallow the shot of tequila; bang the shot glass down on the bar; pick up a wedge of lemon or lime and suck on it; smack your lips and say, "Ahhhh." If this is too hard-core for you, remember that tequila also mixes well with fruit juice.

All tequila sold in the United States is produced in Mexico. The most common brand name by far is José Cuervo, made by a company that produces both white and gold tequila. Some tequila is sold with a small worm in the bottom of the bottle. Rumor has it that anyone who eats this worm will experience hallucinations, but actually it's drinking all that tequila in an attempt to reach the worm that causes strange visions. Don't be fooled.

Whiskey

Whiskey is a dark liquor made by distilling the fermented mash of rye, barley, corn, or wheat. The dark color is the result of aging in barrels. The vast majority of whiskey sold in the United States is made here or in Scotland, Ireland, or Canada.

Rye Whiskey

This whiskey is made from a blend of grains composed of at least 51 percent rye. It is the most widely consumed whiskey in the United States and Canada. Rye is a blended whiskey combined with neutral grain spirits and bottled at 80 proof or higher. Some of the better-known brands of rye whiskey are: Old Thompsons (U.S.A.), Fleishman's (U.S.A.), Seagram's 7 (U.S.A.), Seagram's V.O. (Canada), Canadian Club (Canada), Crown Royal (Canada), and Kennedy's (Canada).

Bourbon Whiskey

Named for Bourbon County, Kentucky, where it was first produced, bourbon is made from a combination of grains containing at least 51 percent corn. It is aged for at least two years in charred-oak barrels. All bourbon is made in the United States and cannot be called bourbon unless it comes from Bourbon County, Kentucky. Some well-known brands of Bourbon are Wild Turkey, Old Taylor, Early Times, Jim Beam, Hiram Walker, Ten High, and Old Grand-Dad.

Some people refer to Jack Daniel's and George Dickel

as bourbon. They are sorely mistaken. The word "bourbon" does not appear on either of these labels, and for good reason. These two brands—fine liquors, by the way—are actually sour mash whiskeys made in Tennessee.

Scotch Whisky

Scotch whisky (spelled whiskey in the United States and Canada) is produced only in Scotland. It can't be called Scotch unless it comes from Scotland—got it? Most Scotch sold in bars in the United States is blended, meaning that malt whisky (whisky distilled from malted barley) is combined with grain whisky. Legend has it that the first person to blend whiskies was a Scotsman named Andrew Usher.

Scotch gets its unique taste from Scottish barley and from a distilling process that utilizes pot stills heated by peat fires. The majority of Scotch sold in the United States has been aged eight or twelve years, although some of it has been aged longer. It must be aged at least eight years, however. Some popular brands of blended Scotches are Passport, Teacher's, Ballantines, Dewar's White Label, J&B, Cutty Sark, Johnnie Walker Black (aged twelve years), Johnnie Walker Red (eight years), and Chivas Regal (twelve years).

Unblended, or single-malt, Scotch is consumed primarily by Scotch purists. It has a much heavier, smokier taste than the blended varieties. Single-malt Scotch seems to be increasing in popularity as more and more people are acquiring a taste for it, or pretend that they are. There must be a thousand single-malt distilleries in Scotland, each claiming a distinctive taste due to the special barley they use, the way their peat burns in their ancient stone building, and so forth. Some brand-names of single malts are Glenlivet, Glenfiddich, Macallan 12, Macallan 18, Laphroaig, Knockando, Pinch, Singleton, and Glenmerengue—and the list goes on. Every family in Scotland seems to have its own distillery.

Irish Whiskey

This whiskey is similar to Scotch, but it's made in Ireland. The two most popular brands sold in the United States are Jameson and Old Bushmills.

Cognac

Cognac is a brandy (grape-based liquor) from the Cognac region in France. It is generally consumed straight up in a brandy snifter. In fact, this is what a brandy snifter is designed for; it makes you stick your nose right in there and breathe in the strong aroma of a fine cognac while you drink it.

Cognac is generally expensive and can range anywhere from six dollars to eighty dollars (Louis XIII) a shot. The letters VS or VSOP may appear on the label; they stand for "very special" and "very special old pale." VSOP is the finer and more expensive category. The cognac labeled XO is one step above VSOP in quality and price. Rémy Martin also has a Napoleon category, which is considered finer than VSOP. The finer the cognac, the higher the price and the smoother it should be.

Any drinking establishment worth its salt will carry the following brands—to display, at least, even if the clientele can't afford to buy them: Rémy Martin VSOP, Hennessy VS, Hennessy VSOP, Courvoisier VSOP, Martell VSOP.

The makers of cognac and its sister, Armagnac, a brandy from the Armagnac region in France, use techniques passed down and perfected over centuries—including costly and time-consuming double-distilling in specially constructed round pots—to produce a fine, consistent product. Cognac should be consumed straight up and not mixed with anything. Some people will drink fine cognac mixed with Coke or ginger ale. This, in my opinion, is a crime against nature and should be punishable by death.

TWO

ALL ABOUT LIQUEURS

BASIC LIQUEURS

A liqueur (pronounced li kûr) is a sweetened alcoholic beverage, sometimes referred to as a cordial. There are countless varieties of liqueurs flavored with everything from almonds to melons to chocolate. The so-called fruit brandies, for example, are really not brandies at all, but fruit-flavored liqueurs. In essence, any alcoholic beverage with a sugar content of more than 14 percent can be considered a liqueur.

Liqueurs are usually served straight up in cordial glasses or brandy snifters as after-dinner drinks, or they are mixed with other ingredients in cocktails. A typical drinking establishment will stock the following liqueurs:

Apple brandy, an apple-flavored liqueur

Amaretto, an almond-flavored liqueur (Italy)

Anisette, an anise-flavored liqueur (Italy)

Apricot brandy, an apricot-flavored liqueur

Baileys Irish Cream, a whiskey- and mint-flavored cream liqueur (Ireland)

Benedictine, an herb-flavored liqueur developed by French monks (France)

B&B, a mixture of Benedictine and brandy (France)

Blackberry brandy, a blackberry-flavored liqueur

Blue curaçao, an orange-flavored liqueur, blue in color

Butterscotch schnapps, a butterscotch-flavored liqueur

Cherry brandy, a cherry-flavored liqueur

Chambord, a raspberry-flavored liqueur (France)

Chartreuse, an herb-flavored liqueur, either green or yellow in color (France)

Cinnamon schnapps, a cinnamon-flavored liqueur

Cointreau, an orange-flavored liqueur (France)

Crème de bananes, a banana-flavored liqueur

Crème de cacao, a brandy-based white or dark liqueur flavored with cacao beans

Crème de cassis, a bitter red liqueur flavored with black currants (France)

Crème de menthe, a mint-flavored white or green liqueur

Crème de noyau, an almond-flavored pink liqueur (France)

Drambuie, a Scotch-based herbal liqueur (Scotland)

Frangelico, a hazelnut-flavored liqueur (Italy)

Galliano, an herb-flavored yellow liqueur (Italy)

Goldwasser, an herb-flavored liqueur flecked with bits of real gold leaf (Germany)

Grand Marnier, a grape-based liqueur flavored with oranges (France)

Irish Mist, a whiskey-based liqueur (Ireland)

Kahlúa, a coffee-flavored dark liqueur (Mexico)

Kümmel, a caraway-flavored liqueur (Germany)

Metaxa, an herb-flavored caramel-color liqueur (Greece)

Midori, a bright green liqueur flavored with honeydew melon (Japan)

Ouzo, an anise-flavored liqueur (Greece)

Peach brandy, a peach-flavored liqueur

Peppermint schnapps, a clear peppermint-flavored liqueur (Germany)

Peter Herring, a cherry-flavored liqueur (Denmark)

Prunelle, a plum-flavored liqueur (France)

Raspberry brandy, a raspberry-flavored liqueur

Rumple Mintz, a clear, strong (100 proof) peppermint-flavored liqueur (Germany)

Sabra, an orange- and chocolate-flavored liqueur (Israel)

Sambuca, a clear, licorice-flavored liqueur (Italy)

Sloe gin, not gin at all but a red liqueur flavored with sloe berries

Strawberry liqueur, a strawberry-flavored liqueur

Strega, a liqueur flavored with orange peel and spices (Italy)

Tia Maria, a coffee-flavored liqueur (Jamaica)

Triple Sec, a clear, orange-flavored liqueur

Vandermint, a chocolate- and mint-flavored liqueur (Netherlands)

Yukon Jack, a strong (100 proof) amber liqueur (Canada)

THREE

BEER

Beer is made by fermenting and aging a mixture of cereal grains and hops. (Hops are the flower clusters of vines similar to the mulberry.) Historical records indicate that beer was probably the first alcoholic beverage invented by man. (Wasn't that beer they were drinking in *Beowulf*?) The main varieties of beer are lager, light, stout, ale, porter, bock, pilsner, and malt.

Lager

Lager (pronounced *lah*-grr) is the most popular type of beer in the United States. It is typically pale in color and heavily carbonated. Brewed by slow fermentation and stored in refrigerated rooms while aging, it has an alcohol content between 3 percent and 4.5 percent. Budweiser, Coors, and Rolling Rock are popular American lagers.

Light Beer

Developed in the United States, which, incidentally, is the largest producer of beer in the world, light beer has fewer calories than regular beer. It can be a pilsner or a lager—"light" pertains only to the caloric content, not the color. It has become so popular in recent years that all major producers of beer have a light product on their roster. Some claim that light beer is responsible for drawing women into the beer market in significant numbers, but this is a sexist statement that assumes women are more conscious about calories than men. Plenty of men drink light beer. Bud Light and Miller Lite are the two giants of the light beer industry.

Pilsner

Pilsner beer is golden in color with a strong hops flavor. It has an alcohol content of about 5 percent. Pilsner originated in Czechoslovakia, but today the term "pilsner" applies to many brands of beer. Pilsner Urquel is the real McCoy, especially good on tap, but rare. If you are lucky enough to work in a place that carries this product, serve it in an unchilled mug for best results.

Ale

Technically ale is not a beer, but its own distinct category of beverage. Ale is made using a shorter brewing process. Ale originated in England, where it is consumed at room temperature. It is copper in color and much heavier and more bitter than beer. It also has a much stronger hops flavor and a higher alcohol content. Bass Ale is the standard by which all the others are measured, although there are countless varieties due to the recent explosion in micro-breweries.

Stout

A heavy-bodied brew made from roasted malt and hops, stout is a very dark and thick brew. Stout is the national drink of Ireland, where it is consumed at room temperature. If you've been in an Irish bar you've seen the customers drinking Guinness stout in pint glasses. Looks like motor oil with a thick, creamy head. A couple pints of that and you'll be singing "When Irish Eyes Are Smiling" right along with the band!

Porter

Porter is a dark, heavy ale that is very sweet and not very common. Like stout, it is consumed at room temperature. Many microbreweries put out a regular porter or a honey porter on a seasonal basis.

Bock

Originally from Germany, bock beer is a heavy, sediment-filled beer obtained when the barrels are first tapped. In other words, it comes right off the bottom of the barrel. It is dark brown in color with an alcohol content of about 6 percent. Sam Adams bock is as good as it comes.

Malt Liquor

The heavy beer commonly referred to as malt liquor is brewed from fermented malt, which is grain (usually barley) soaked in water until it sprouts. Malt liquor has a very high alcohol content and is marketed as a cheap way to get loaded. Colt 45 is a popular malt liquor.

More About Beer

There are many types and brands of beer on the market today. A drinking establishment may have one or two brands for sale or it may feature more than a hundred. Recently there has been a proliferation of microbreweries, small local breweries that produce several varieties of hand-crafted beer. The trend is moving away from the more generic, homogeneous product of the giant beer companies to the tastier, more distinctive products of these small breweries. Because they produce in relatively small batches, the microbreweries are able to alter their recipes and come out with seasonal and flavored beers such as winter brew and pumpkin- and spice-flavored beer.

A by-product of this increase in the number of microbreweries is the emergence of the beer snob, a close relative of the wine snob. The beer snob is the customer who asks for a taste of each of the beers on tap before buying. He then swirls the beer around in the glass, sniffs the bouquet, takes a teeny-weeny sip, swishes it around in his mouth, and pronounces it "on the bitter side" or "hoppy." Notice that he finishes every drop of each sample you give him, even the ones he claims to detest. That way he consumes about half a glass of free beer.

Beer comes in bottles or kegs, which are 13-gallon (50 liter) metal barrels. These kegs are pressurized with carbon dioxide, and the beer is run to the taps, or spigots, through plastic tubes called lines. True beer connoisseurs prefer beer from kegs because it is less pasteurized and generally has fewer added preservatives. The lines that carry the beer from the kegs to the taps must be cleaned regularly, however. Often the kegs are stored in a refrigerated room some distance from the taps, so these lines can be quite long. There are professionals who specialize in this type of service. They use special pumps and solvents to flush out the entire system.

Beer contains yeast, and yeast is alive. Living things grow and multiply, and you don't necessarily want to drink these little creatures with your beer. Some drinking establishments have the lines flushed every couple weeks; others *never* have the lines flushed. Wonder why the draft beer at your favorite corner pub tastes a little funky?

FOUR

WINE

As a professional bartender you may find that wine is either a very important aspect of your job or only a minor element. A corner bar may carry only a cheap white wine in one-gallon jugs, while a fancy restaurant may have a wine list with a hundred different varieties. As a professional bartender, however, you have to know at least a little about wine, so here we go.

All wines are produced by fermenting grapes. (Fermentation is the transformation of grape juice by enzymes in the absence of oxygen.) The different characteristics of wines are due to differences in the grapes used, the climate and soil where the grapes are grown, the time of harvest, the fermentation process, the aging process, the type of wood in which the wine is aged, and the skill of the vintner.

Wines can be divided into three major types: table wine, sparkling wine, and fortified wine.

TABLE WINE

Table wine can be white, rosé or red.

White wine, which is pale to golden in color, is made by separating the dark grape skins from the grapes right after they are crushed.

Rosé wine, which is pink or "blush" in color, is made by allowing the skins to soak in the grape juice for several days after crushing.

Red wine, which is dark red to purple in color, is made by allowing the skins to soak in the grape juice for several weeks. (The skin of the grape contains a chemical that helps in reducing blood cholesterol, hence the connection between red wine and reduced risk of heart attack.)

All three varieties are aged first in wooden casks, then in bottles. Most wines will end up with an alcohol content of 10 percent to 14 percent.

All wines fall somewhere on the spectrum between dry and sweet. Dry wine has a lower sugar content; sweet wines contain more sugar.

Sophisticated wine connoisseurs can identify specific regions and vintages of wines. (The vintage year, or the year the grapes were harvested, is very important because grape crops vary from year to year.) Wine experts employ an entire vocabulary to describe the taste, aroma, bouquet, body, and color of wine. They use words like *bold, steely, nutty, earthy, fruity, oaky, pretentious,* and *overbearing.* Though it may seem like nonsense when you see these experts gargling with the wine and spitting it into buckets, the adjectives they're using actually mean something, and— believe it or not—each of these experts actually understands what the others are talking about.

Most wines sold in the United States come from France, Spain, Italy, Germany, and California, although you do occasionally see wines today from Chile, Australia, and Rhode Island.

French wines are named for regions where they are made. Bordeaux, Burgundy, Loire, and Rhône, for instance, are all wines of France. Germany is famous for Rhine wines, while Italy is known for Chianti and Valpolicella (reds) and Soave (white). California wines—chardonnay and sauvignon blanc (whites), white zinfandel (rosé), and merlot (red)—are sold nearly everywhere now.

Whenever possible, wine bottles should be stored in a horizontal position in order to keep the corks wet. A wet cork will remain swollen and maintain the water-tight seal. Bottles should be kept in a cool, dark place at 50–60° F. Before refrigeration was invented, wine was usually stored in a cellar, hence the term "wine cellar."

How to Serve Wine

White and rosé wines should be chilled in a refrigerator or by placing the bottle in ice. Red wines should be served at room temperature and allowed to "breathe" for an hour before serving. (You let the wine breathe by removing the cork.) Heaven forbid someone should drink red wine that's been holding its breath!

When you serve a house wine by the glass, simply pour it and give it to the customer as you would any other beverage. To serve a bottle, follow this procedure: Show the label to the person who ordered the wine and let him or her verify that you pulled the right bottle out of the wine cooler. Remove the cork from the bottle without breaking it and pour a small amount into the customer's glass. (In the past it was always a man who tasted the wine, the theory being that if it was bad, he would suffer chivalrously. Today, however, you should pour the taste for the person who ordered the wine.) The customer will smell it and taste it to see if it is okay. Sometimes, though not very often, wine will go bad in the bottle and turn to vinegar. That is the reason for tasting—to see if the wine has gone bad, not to see if one likes the wine or not. No customer should ever return the wine just because he or she doesn't like it.

Once the person has tasted the wine and given you a nod of approval, pour a glass for each person and leave the cork next to the bottle. Some wine drinkers like to examine the cork, believing this gives them insight into the nature of the wine. Others like to take the cork home.

Volumes and volumes have been written on this subject by experts who have devoted their lives to the study of wine. A complete, in-depth discussion of wines is beyond the scope of this book, but as a professional bartender, you should be familiar with the wines that are available at your establishment. You might also want to learn a few adjectives to throw around to impress the snobs. Learn which wines complement certain foods, too.

Sparkling Wine

Sparkling wines are carbonated as a result of a second fermentation process that occurs after the wine has been bottled. Sparkling wine is produced in almost every wine-producing country, including the United States. The word "champagne" is often used today to denote any sparkling wine, but this is technically incorrect. Like bourbon and cognac, champagne is a regional product—sparkling wine from the Champagne region of France and only from the Champagne region of France. Everything else is sparkling wine. To refer to a sparkling wine from New York State as champagne is an affront to wine connoisseurs the world over. It's like pointing at a Ford and saying, "Boy, look at that Porsche!" All champagnes are sparkling wines, but not all sparkling wines are champagnes.

Sparkling wine can be labeled brut, or extra dry, meaning there is very little added sugar. Sparkling wine should always be served well chilled, preferably packed on ice.

Take a close look at a sparkling wine bottle and you will notice that the bottom has a deep indentation. This shape isn't for looks; it makes the bottle stronger. The glass is thicker and heavier than that of a regular wine bottle, and the cork is secured to the neck of the bottle with a wire cage. The sparkling wine bottle is designed in this fashion to withstand tremendous pressure. For this reason, you must be careful when you remove the cork! Never point the cork at yourself or at a customer. Always keep your hand or a towel over the cork while removing it; sometimes a cork will explode out of the bottle as soon as you twist off the wire cage. When you remove the cork, and it makes that festive pop, keep the bottle tilted at forty-five degrees so that the sparkling wine will not overflow.

Serve sparkling wine in either saucer champagne glasses or fluted glasses. Sparkling wine tends to go flat quickly once it is opened, so it should be recorked immediately, using a special rubber cork designed for this purpose. If you jam a regular cork back into the bottle, keep it on ice pointed in a safe direction because it might fly out at any time. The time-honored way to keep sparkling wine from going flat is to drink it quickly.

Sparkling wine is being used more often in mixed cocktails, most notably the mimosa, so it is gradually becoming a standard item behind the typical bar.

FORTIFIED WINE

Fortified wines are those wines to which other ingredients, usually brandies, have been added. This is done during the fermentation process to alter the character and increase the alcohol content of the wine. Sherry, vermouth, port and Madeira are well-known fortified wines.

Sherry

Brandy is added to sherry during the production process. *Dry sherry* is light, and is generally served as a before-dinner drink, or *aperitif* (pronounced a-pair-i-*teef*) to stimulate the appetite. *Sweet sherry* and *cream sherry*, which are dark and sweet, are usually served as after-dinner drinks. Two popular brands of sherry found in most drinking establishments are Harveys Bristol Cream and Dry Sack.

Port

During the fermentation process, brandy is added to port, which is then aged. *Ruby port* is less than twelve years old, *tawny port* is between twelve and fifteen years old, and *vintage port* is over fifteen years old. When pouring port, you must decant the bottle very carefully so as not to give the customer a glass filled with sediment.

Vermouth

Vermouth is an herbal wine to which brandy has been added during the fermentation process. *Dry vermouth*, which is pale yellow, is used in this country primarily as an ingredient in martinis, although some people drink it over ice as an aperitif. *Sweet vermouth* is dark red with a very sweet taste and is used primarily as an ingredient in manhattans, although some people drink it over ice as an after-dinner drink.

MADEIRA

This rich fortified white wine is from Madeira, a group of volcanic islands off the northwest coast of Africa and under the government of Portugal. It is usually served as an after-dinner drink.

Most drinking establishments also carry Dubonnet, a sweet red fortified wine, and Lillet, which may be either white (dry) or red (sweet). Both of these wines are products of France, where aperitifs got their name.

FIVE

FRUITS, JUICES, AND OTHER INGREDIENTS

Contrary to popular belief, bartending is not all glamour. In most drinking establishments the bartenders will be required to arrive at work several hours before the opening shift, not so they can drink coffee, browse through the paper and engage in leisurely discussion, but so they can hurry up and get the bar ready before the first customers come barreling through the front door.

GARNISHES

Garnishes are used in cocktails to add flavor and to provide decoration. Preparing garnishes eats up a good part of the bartender's setup time. For this task, you'll need a sharp knife, which is safer and faster than a dull one, and a clean cutting board, preferably made of a synthetic material that you can clean with bleach once in a while.

Garnishes are usually kept in specially designed metal

or plastic trays with removable plastic cups and a clear plastic lid.

Lime Wedges

To prepare lime wedges, you simply cut a lime in half lengthwise, then cut each piece in half again lengthwise. Hold two pieces together with the skin side up and cut them in half crosswise again to make the wedges. One lime will yield eight wedges. You can then squeeze the lime wedge as you drop it into the cocktail.

An alternate method is to cut a lime into quarters or sixths, make a slit in each section, and place a piece on the rim of each glass so the customers can squeeze or not squeeze according to their preference.

Cocktails made with tonic water or Rose's lime juice should always be served with a lime wedge garnish. Often a customer will ask for a cocktail with a "twist of lime." What they usually mean is a wedge of lime.

Lime Wheels

To prepare lime wheels, cut the ends off a lime to expose a fair amount of the pulp. Make a slice down the length of the lime about one-third to one-half inch deep. Cut cross sections of the lime to get lime wheels, making each one about one-quarter inch thick. One lime will yield five or six wheels. Cut a small notch in each wheel so it can be hung on the rim of a cocktail glass.

Lime wedges are decorative garnishes used on many exotic cocktails, including the frozen margarita, and sometimes used in place of lime wedges.

Lemon Twists

Prepare lemon twists by first cutting the ends off a lemon to expose a fair amount of the meat. Then place your thumb on the bowl part of a bar spoon, force the edge of the spoon between the meat of the lemon and the white layer of the skin. Work your way around the lemon, then flip it over and repeat the process on the other end. Now the meat is totally separated from the skin and can be pushed out in one piece leaving a whole shell of skin. Cut the skin lengthwise into strips about one-third inch wide and one and a half to two inches long. An average-size lemon will yield about fifteen twists.

An alternate way to make lemon twists is to cut off the ends of the lemon to expose the meat and then score the lemon lengthwise using just the very tip of the knife. Rotate the lemon until you've scored it all the way around. Place the whole lemon in the garnish tray and peel the twists off one by one as you need them. The twists will stay fresh longer this way, but they may not be as uniform.

Watch closely while you twist a lemon twist and you will see a spray of tiny droplets shoot from the yellow side of the skin. This is the oil of the lemon, which will add aroma and flavor to a cocktail.

The proper way to garnish a cocktail with a lemon twist is to hold the strip of rind over the cocktail and twist it to release the oil in such a way that the oil shoots down into the drink. Then rub the yellow outer part of the twist all the way around the rim of the cocktail glass and drop the twist into the drink. Twist, rub, drop. Check the recipes to be sure which drinks get a twist.

Orange Slices

Prepare orange slices by first cutting off both ends of the orange to expose a fair amount of the meat. Then cut the orange in half lengthwise, place each half skin side up on the cutting board, and cut it crosswise into slices shaped like half moons, each about one-third of an inch thick. An average orange will yield twelve slices.

Cherries

The most common cherry garnishes are Maraschino cherries, which are bright red and very sweet. They are dropped directly into the cocktail.

Olives

Large Spanish olives stuffed with pimientos, which are sold to drinking establishments in one-gallon glass jars, are the preferred garnish for martinis. You simply spear the olive with a toothpick or sword pick and drop it into the cocktail. Some establishments use olives stuffed with almonds or anchovies instead of pimientos.

An excellent bartender pick-me-up is an olive with a few drops of Tabasco sauce poured into the hole with the pimiento. Eat one every two hours to help fight drowsiness and aid in concentration.

Cocktail Onions

Tiny white onions are used in only one cocktail—the Gibson. In fact, it is only the onions that differentiate a Gibson from a martini. Otherwise the two cocktails are exactly the same. A small jar of cocktail onions should last a long time in a typical drinking establishment.

To garnish a cocktail with onions, spear four or five tiny onions with toothpick or sword pick and drop the pick into cocktail.

Celery Stalks

Prepare this garnish by trimming and washing the celery stalks. Store them in a container with cold water in the bottom. The stalks will suck up the water and stay nice and stiff. If you forget to put the water in, they will turn limp and rubbery in a matter of hours.

Celery is used to garnish the Bloody Mary and its relatives, the Virgin Mary, Bloody Caesar, and Bloody Maria, and to provide an edible stirrer.

Pineapple Slices

To prepare pineapple slices, first cut the top and bottom off a fresh pineapple to expose a fair amount of the meat. Then cut the pineapple in half lengthwise. Place both halves skin side up on the cutting board and cut them in half lengthwise again. Turn each pineapple quarter over and make an incision in the meat about one-half inch deep down the entire length. This will be the notch used to hang each slice on the rim of the glass. Turn the pineapple quarter back over, skin side up, and cut cross sections to get triangular pineapple slices. An average pineapple will yield about thirty-two slices.

Pineapple slices are used primarily on frozen drinks and other tropical cocktails.

Butterflies

A butterfly garnish is an orange slice wrapped around a cherry and speared with toothpick or sword pick.

Flags

To make flags you'll need pineapple slices or orange slices and cherries. Pin one cherry to the outside rim of each fruit slice using a toothpick or sword pick.

Garnishing Tips

Make sure that all of your garnishes are fresh. It does nothing for your reputation when you serve a drink garnished with a petrified orange slice from the Paleozoic era. When there is no time to cut fresh fruit, or there is none in the house, fill the plastic cups in the garnish trays with water and allow the dried-out fruit wedges to soak. That will make them *look* fresher and more appetizing.

Make sure the garnish trays are emptied and washed out every night as part of the routine, or one day you'll open the garnish tray in front of a customer and a swarm of fruit flies will magically appear.

Keep your knife sharp, pay attention, and don't hurry when cutting fruit. It can be tedious work, especially if you have to cut up an entire box of limes, but you must keep your mind and your eyes on what you're doing. A cut is not only painful, but the bloody Band-Aid on your finger will look bad in front of customers and will hamper your ability to do your job. If it's deep enough, it may keep you out of work.

JUICES AND JUICE MIXTURES

A typical drinking establishment will stock any number of juices and juice mixtures to be used in drinks. Tomato, orange, grapefruit, cranberry, and pineapple juice are standard items, as is sour mix.

Also called lemon mix, sour mix is a very sweet lemon-flavored juice used primarily in drinks such as the whiskey sour and vodka collins. It is usually sold to bars in powdered form and then mixed with water and stored in one-gallon containers. It takes the place of the "one teaspoon of sugar and the juice of one lemon" in the old drink recipes.

To make up a batch of sour mix, fill a one-gallon container—usually a cleaned-out cherry jar—halfway to the top with water, add the bag of powdered mix, cover the jar, and shake well, then fill it to the top with water and cover and shake well again. If you put the powder in first, a certain amount of it will adhere to the bottom of the container like glue. No matter how hard you shake, the rest of the mixture will be weak, and customers will be returning their whiskey sours all night complaining that they taste watery.

RealLemon is also found behind some bars. This is

lemon juice concentrate, which is different from lemon mix. It comes in small bottles ready to use.

Those establishments equipped with electric blenders will also have piña colada mix and several other fruit juice mixers. Used to make piña coladas and several other exotic drinks, piña colada mix is made by combining one part cream of coconut with three parts pineapple juice. Prepared piña colada mix is sold in cans; the ingredients are also sold separately and then mixed by the bartender. It is best to soak those little cans of cream of coconut in hot water before mixing with pineapple juice. Otherwise the cream will coagulate and be hard to mix.

Another fruit mixer is strawberry puree, which is used primarily to make frozen strawberry daiquiris (pronounced *dack*-er-ees). To make this mixer, you simply let some frozen sliced strawberries thaw, place them in a blender, and puree them for just a couple seconds until they're smooth. In an emergency, if you run out of puree in the middle of a busy shift, you can run a container of frozen berries through the dishwasher a couple times, open it, pry off partly thawed chunks with the bar spoon, and blend them with a little hot water.

OTHER INGREDIENTS

Behind the bar in a typical drinking establishment you will find numerous other mixed-drink ingredients, among which will probably be most of those described below.

Milk, Cream, and Half and Half

Milk and cream are used in many popular cocktails, including the sombrero and the white Russian. They must be fresh and cold.

Grenadine and Rose's Lime Juice

Grenadine is a nonalcoholic red syrup used to sweeten and color many popular cocktails. Real grenadine used to be made from the juice of pomegranates, but now it is artificially flavored. (Interesting fact: the Grenadines are a chain of six hundred British islands in the West Indies).

Rose's lime juice is watery lime-flavored juice used to add color and sweetness to the gimlet and other cocktails.

Angostura Bitters

A dark brown liquid flavored with roots and herbs, angostura bitters is used very sparingly in cocktails such at the Old Fashioned to add flavor and color. It is sold to drinking establishments in 8- or 12-ounce bottles that should last for a long, long time. A few dashes of bitters in a glass of soda water is a time-honored remedy for an upset stomach. Note, however, that bitters contains alcohol.

Bloody Mary Ingredients

There are several different recipes for Bloody Mary mix, but most will include salt, pepper, Worcestershire sauce, Tabasco sauce, celery salt, horseradish, and, of course, tomato juice.

Each of these ingredients may be added as each individual drink is made, or they may be premixed. There are two ways to mix Bloody Mary ingredients. One way is to mix together all the ingredients in the correct proportions, including tomato juice, and store it in one-gallon containers. Another way is to mix together all the ingredients *except* the tomato juice, making a base, which is then spooned into the glass as needed.

Mixing together all the ingredients, including the tomato juice, ahead of time is the most efficient method, but the ingredients tend to settle to the bottom of the big storage containers and the shelf life is shorter because tomato juice goes bad quickly.

I think using the base is the best way to go because it's quick and easy to make the drinks, the Bloody Marys will be consistent from bartender to bartender, and the base can be stored in a small container and will have a long shelf life.

Here is a recipe for a quart of base that will make 35 to 40 Bloody Marys:

> 3 cups horseradish
> ½ cup Worcestershire sauce
> ⅓ cup Tabasco sauce
> 2 tablespoons pepper
> 1½ teaspoons salt
> 1 teaspoon celery salt

Coarse Salt and Nutmeg

Some establishments serve a lot of margaritas and will carry a special extra-coarse salt to be used on the rims of the glasses. Special devices designed for this purpose hold a moist sponge and have a compartment for the salt. If you don't have one of these devices, moisten the rim of the glass with a lime wedge and sprinkle salt on it from a shaker or press the rim into a dish of salt.

You should keep a little shaker of ground nutmeg at hand so that you can sprinkle some on the surface of creamy cocktails such as the brandy Alexander, for decoration.

Those are the basic juices and other ingredients you will find behind the bar in a typical drinking establishment. Of course, if you are so fortunate as to land a job in a bar with a whole separate menu of exotic drinks, you will undoubtedly have access to additional juices, mixes, and ingredients—chocolate sauce, whipped cream, bananas, vanilla extract, cinnamon, cucumbers, dill pickles, and who knows what else. It's gone too far, if you ask me. You're on your own with all that stuff.

One final recommendation: at the beginning of each shift, check all your juices and other ingredients for freshness. This means smelling and tasting each juice. Juices can spoil in a matter of hours. Milk can turn to cheese. Pineapple juice will separate. Tomato juice may get fizzy. It is embarrassing to serve a cocktail and have the customer gag and spit it back into the glass. That can ruin your whole day.

Also, keep the plastic juice bottles clean. They need to be emptied out and cleaned every night, not just refilled and refilled ad infinitum. This willingness to take the extra step is what separates the professional bartenders from the amateurs. Customers notice small details. That big tipper is going to decide against a second Bloody Mary when she sees that crusty, clogged spout on the tomato juice container that hasn't been cleaned since Reagan was in office. Cleaning is part of your job. Do your job.

SIX

TOOLS OF THE TRADE

Behind every bar you will find basically the same equipment. These are the tools of the trade, and as a professional bartender you should be intimately familiar with all of them.

MIXING EQUIPMENT

The basic equipment used to mix cocktails has remained the same since cocktails first became popular in the 1920s.

Shaker Cups

Sometimes referred to as mixing cups, these stainless-steel cups are placed over glasses while cocktails are being shaken. The 12-ounce shaker cup is usually placed directly over a highball glass. The 24-ounce cup is placed over a mixing glass.

Mixing Glass

Thick, sturdy mixing glasses with a 16-ounce capacity are used to "build" certain cocktails. Martinis and manhattans, for instance, are built in a mixing glass. A large mixing cup is sometimes placed over the mixing glass; the drink is then shaken and poured from the mixing glass, ice and all, into the serving glass. In other instances, a cocktail is built in the mixing glass, stirred with a bar spoon, and then strained into the serving glass.

Bar Spoon

This long-handled metal spoon is used for stirring drinks in the mixing glass, spooning in ingredients, floating liquors, and making lemon twists.

Strainer

You will need a metal strainer with a coil spring attached to hold it firmly in place over a mixing glass or shaker cup. After shaking or stirring a cocktail with ice, you will pour the drink through this strainer into a cocktail glass so that it can be served straight up and ice cold.

Jigger

A jigger is a device used to measure the amount of liquor poured into a drink. It is usually made of stainless steel and shaped like two small cones connected at the bottom so that one glass is always upside down. One part usually holds 1¼ ounces, and the other holds 2 ounces, though some jiggers have different capacities. Sometimes a standard 1½-ounce shot glass is used in place of a jigger. Liquor is measured into the jigger or shot glass and then poured into the cocktail glass or mixing glass.

Some establishments allow the bartenders to "free pour." This means the bartenders add the alcohol to the cocktail without measuring it in a jigger; they rely instead on an internal count to arrive at the proper amount. Free pouring allows bartenders to work faster, because they can pour with both hands instead of using one to hold the jigger, and it looks fancier. The drinks will not be consistent from one bartender to the next, however, or from one night to the next. Cocktails may be too strong or too weak, and management will have much less control over the liquor cost.

Can and Bottle Opener

Most bars have heavy-duty openers that punch extra-large holes in juice cans and remove bottle caps easily.

Corkscrew

A handheld lever-type corkscrew with a small folding knife on one end is preferred. The type that fits over the neck of the bottle and has two arms that rise as the screw is turned into the cork is foolproof, but it's bulky to carry around in your pocket and it's considered amateurish by real pros.

In some establishments you will find a large lever-operated corkscrew made of chrome-plated steel that resembles a medieval torture device. To use this device, you hold the bottle in place, pull the wooden lever down and then up, and the mechanical screw bores into the cork and removes it in a fraction of a second. With this contraption, you can open an entire case of wine in less than five minutes!

Ice Scoop

Always use a metal or plastic scoop to place ice in a cocktail glass or blender. Using your hand is both unsanitary and unprofessional. Do not scoop up the ice with the glass itself. If it breaks, you will be faced with the time-consuming task of melting down all the ice and refilling the ice bin.

Extended Drain Stopper

This rubber stopper with an extended metal tube is a simple but indispensable device. When the stopper is in place, you can fill the sink with water before it begins to run down the tube. That way, the faucet can be left trickling so the water in the sink will circulate and remain clean, a necessary condition for proper rinsing of the mixing equipment.

Speed Pourers

Speed pourers are plastic metal spouts that are inserted into the liquor bottles to control the flow of liquor. These devices allow the bartender to direct the flow of liquor into the jigger or cocktail glass with a maximum of speed and a minimum of spillage.

Some speed pourers out there actually measure a shot of liquor automatically, but these things are unwieldy and unattractive.

When pouring liquor, hold the neck of the bottle in such a way that your forefinger overlaps the speed pourer. This helps you guide the liquor, and it looks professional. It also prevents the speed pourer from slipping out of the bottle. That rarely happens, but when it does, it makes a mess and is very embarrassing.

Muddler

A muddler is a small wooden club about six inches long. Shaped like a baseball bat, it is used to mash, or muddle, the fruit in the bottom of an Old Fashioned glass. Not to be confused with the real baseball bat that is kept behind the bar in certain establishments to muddle those customers who get out of line.

Cutting Board and Knife

These tools are necessary for preparing fresh garnishes.

Plastic Juice Bottles and Rack

You will need specially designed plastic juice bottles with removable necks and removable color-coded spouts. You'll place these bottles in a specific order in a specially designed rack, which is recessed into the ice bin to keep the juices chilled and to give you instant access.

Sip Sticks, Swizzle Sticks, and Straws

These tiny straws or stirrers are used in mixed drinks. Any cocktail served over ice automatically gets a sip stick. Originally designed so women could sip cocktails without smearing their lipstick. Many frozen drinks and tall cocktails are served with standard-size straws.

Toothpicks and Sword Picks

Olives are threaded on toothpicks or sword picks before being placed in martinis. Picks are also used for butterfly and flag garnishes, in which fruits are pinned together.

Beverage Napkins or Coasters

Beverage napkins are used to protect the bar as well as to greet customers and signify that they are being waited on. Customers can also use them to jot down phone numbers, map out directions, or draw up contracts. Most establishments have their logo on the napkins or on specially designed disposable coasters.

Bar Towel or Bar Rag

The small white towel used by bartenders is usually cotton, and traditionally sports a blue stripe. It is used for everything from wiping the bar to polishing bottles to fashioning a tourniquet when you wound yourself while cutting fruit.

Blender

Most drinking establishments today have electric blenders for making the many popular frozen drinks that customers love and bartenders hate. Several of the industrial models on the market are reasonably durable and easy to operate.

Soda System

Almost every drinking establishment today uses a pressurized soda system. This means that the bartender is able to dispense several flavors of soda from a gun located at the mixing station. The standard soda gun has seven buttons labeled *C* (cola), *L* (7UP or Sprite), *Q* (quinine or tonic water), *T* (Tab or diet cola), *G* (ginger ale), *S* (soda water), and *W* (water).

Soda is delivered to the gun by pressurized carbon dioxide stored in large metal canisters. The different sodas are attached to the system between the CO_2 and the gun. The sodas are stored in 5-gallon metal canisters or in cardboard boxes with a plastic bladder inside. These boxes are stackable and disposable. One caution: do not use a knife to cut through the cardboard; you will puncture the bladder and make a mess of titanic proportions.

The soda system is generally maintained by the vendor who provides the product. However, day-to-day maintenance—replacing the boxes of syrup, making sure the CO_2 is active—falls to the bartender. It is a good idea to check the soda containers before a busy shift to see if they need to be replaced. If this is not done, you could find the cola coming out of the gun looking like weak iced tea right in the middle of a busy shift. At least make sure that backup boxes or canisters of syrup are set up nearby for easy changing. Also make sure the box wrench used to change the CO_2 is always attached to the hose.

Beer System

Many drinking establishments have different beers available on tap. This means that the beer is stored in metal kegs, sometimes referred to as half-kegs or barrels. Each keg holds approximately 13 gallons, or 50 liters, of beer.

Beer in kegs must be stored cold, preferably between 42°F (5.5°C) and 45°F (7.2°C). Kegs are sometimes stored in specially designed refrigeration units with the taps right on top. These units sit right behind the bar and usually hold one to three kegs. Drinking establishments that sell several types of tap beer will have a walk-in cooler on the premises where the kegs are stored. The beer is pressurized with carbon dioxide and delivered to the taps at the bar through plastic tubes, or lines.

Taking care of the kegs is the responsibility of the bartender. (And you thought this job involved no heavy lifting?) Take the time when the beer delivery comes to set the kegs up properly, with full backups underneath the tapped kegs. The middle of a busy shift is no time to be in the keg room shifting those heavy kegs around.

Take time in the morning to bleed, or drain, the lines of all the stale beer that has been sitting in there overnight.

When a keg kicks, or runs out of beer, a blast of pressure will shoot out of the tap. If your tap is right at the bar and you're holding a full glass of beer up to the tap when the keg kicks, you may splash beer all over yourself and your customers. This is embarrassing. When a keg is about to kick, the beer will start to come out a little faster and will look flat. Check your kegs ahead of time so you know which ones are ready to kick.

The beer lines should be cleaned regularly by professionals who specialize in this service. Otherwise the beer will start to taste sour, and when you open the taps in the morning, strange globs of black slime may come out.

Tap beer is more difficult to deal with than bottled beer. It's finicky, often it won't pour correctly, and you get a sore back from lifting those heavy kegs. There is a much higher profit margin in tap beer, however, and management likes that, so get used to it.

Glassware

Different drinks call for different glasses. Here are the types of glassware that will be found in a typical drinking establishment.

White Wine Glass   Red Wine Glass   Champagne Saucer   Champagne Tulip

Small Brandy Snifter   Ballon Snifter   Martini Glass   Irish Coffee Glass

Beer Mug   Pilsner Beer Glass   Collins Glass

1½-ounce Shot Glass   4-ounce Rocks Glass   8-ounce Highball Glass

SEVEN

TYPICAL BAR LAYOUT

Although no two drinking establishments will have exactly the same layout behind the bar, most are very similar. Once you become familiar with one layout, it is easy to learn another.

When viewed from the customer's side, a typical bar is rather plain. The bar itself is usually constructed of stained wood, although it could be marble or Formica. Bar stools line the bar, and liquor bottles are displayed on shelves behind the bar. There are stacks of napkins at regular intervals along the bar, along with sip-stick holders and ashtrays. There are taps, or towers, for dispensing the tap beer. A brass handrail may separate the waiters' service station from the rest of the bar.

From the bartender's viewpoint a typical bar will have several drink stations where each bartender makes his drinks. When the bartender is at his station facing the customers, the drink rail will be directly in front of him. This rail is actually a small shelf, slightly below bar level, where glasses are placed while making cocktails. The rail is covered with bar towels or specially designed rubber mats to absorb the spillage.

Within easy reach the bartender will have a garnish tray, sip sticks, large straws, toothpicks or sword picks, and cocktail napkins or coasters. A soda gun will rest in a holster alongside the rail. Directly below the rail is a bin filled with small ice cubes for cocktails. Large ice cubes are not used in bars because they do not pack the glass properly; they leave too much space for the mixer, and cocktails will taste weak.

Specially designed racks recessed into either side of the ice bin hold the plastic juice bottles. Typically there will be plastic bottles of milk, orange juice, cranberry juice, grapefruit juice, pineapple juice, sour mix, and tomato juice. In some establishments you will find old liquor bottles full of juice stored directly in the ice. This practice is frowned upon by most state health departments.

Next to the ice bin will be three small stainless-steel sinks and a drainboard for washing glasses. Ice and leftover cocktails are dumped into the first sink, which should be equipped with a strainer so the sip sticks won't clog the drain. The second sink is filled with soapy water and has cone-shaped brushes attached to the bottom. The glasses are scrubbed on these brushes under water and then rinsed in the third sink, which is filled with clean, circulating water, thanks to an extended-tube drain stopper. The glasses are then placed on the drainboard, a stainless-steel surface with ridges slanting toward the sink, where they await the next cocktail order.

This three-sink method is rapidly being replaced by small, efficient automatic glass washers that save time and are much more sanitary. All the bartender has to do is make sure the spray wand isn't clogged, clean the screen once in a while, and call the service representative if the machine breaks down.

Directly in front of the bartender, at knee level and attached to the front of the ice bin, is the speed rack, also called the well. This is a metal rack that holds those bottles of liquor that are most often used. Many drinking establishments use the cheapest liquor available in the well, hence the term "well liquor" for cheap booze. A typical speed rack will have bottles of vodka, gin, rum, Scotch, bourbon, tequila, Triple Sec, coffee liqueur, sweet vermouth, dry vermouth, grenadine, Rose's lime juice, and any other liquors commonly used in that drinking establishment. The bottles may be grouped according to the bartender's preference, but the standard method is to put all the clear liquors together, all the dark liquors together, and the lime juice and grenadine down at the end.

Behind the bartender is the backbar, the area where bottles are displayed on shelves. These bottles are known as the call liquor because customers call for them by brand name. Bottles on the backbar are grouped together by type of liquor. For example, Tanqueray, Beefeater, Bombay, and Boodles gin will be set up next to each other. The most often used bottles will be in the most accessible locations. The finest and most expensive brands are kept on the uppermost shelf, hence the expression "top shelf liquor."

A typical bar also has a good deal of refrigerator space to store beer, wine, juices, and other perishable items. Bars that sell a lot of bottled beer will often have drop chests—horizontal refrigerators with sliding doors on top. Many bars with beer on tap have glass chillers, refrigerators designed to put frost on beer mugs.

Cocktail glasses are often kept on shelves behind the bar, though they may also hang upside down in racks over the bar. A lot of space is saved by hanging stemmed glassware from overhead racks, but many state health departments frown on this practice because the glasses are exposed to rising cigarette smoke.

A cash register or computer terminal will be located behind the bar, and if you're lucky, you'll have a couple of electric blenders to play with. There will be beer taps, if the establishment sells tap beer. If food is served at the bar there will also be place mats, flatware, condiments, crockery and menus. Chances are there will be at least one TV, maybe even five or six if you work in a sports bar. This means that the remote control will be lying around somewhere. Try not to drop it into the sink. The backup liquor bottles and supplies will also be stored on shelves or in cabinets behind the bar for easy access.

Because most establishments are similar in layout, when you know how to work behind one bar, you can step behind almost any other and be ready to go—once you learn how to work that complex computerized cash register, that is.

EIGHT

Types of Drinking Establishments

The Corner Pub

Corner pubs can be found in every city and town in the United States. These bars are sometimes called beer-and-shot joints because that is what is most often consumed there. You won't get many calls for frozen strawberry daiquiris in the typical corner pub. Chances are there isn't even a blender behind the bar.

These establishments are generally patronized by blue-collar workers. They sometimes open as early as 8:00 A.M., and by 9:00 A.M. the "Breakfast Club" retirees may be lined up on their regular stools waiting for a ball and a beer—a shot of whiskey with a beer chaser—to start the day off right.

If any food is served at all, it will usually be lunch fare. There will be a rush of business at lunchtime and a rush of after-work drinkers, but you'll have a lot of downtime in between. Do not be deceived by the look of the working-class clientele; members of the humble proletariat are often the best tippers. These people understand what it means to work for a living.

In some corner pubs you will find a baseball bat behind the bar. This may be an indication that you are working in a "bucket o' blood"—in other words, a rough joint. Some bartenders enjoy the thrill of working in a place where drunken brawls, stabbings, and shootings are a nightly occurrence. Others do not.

To bartend in a corner pub you must relate well to the clientele. The customers generally come from the local area, and the regulars may come in once a week, a couple times a week, every day, or even twice a day.

Bartending·is relatively uncomplicated in the corner pub because beer and simple drinks make up the majority of the orders. Customer relations are more important here than in, say, a high-volume nightclub. If you don't mind the retired war veteran bending your ear with the same story a dozen times—then by all means work in a corner pub. You'll make a decent living.

THE NIGHTCLUB

Nightclubs are found primarily in and around large cities. They are likely to go in and out of fashion very quickly. One month the club is mobbed every night, the next month it is no longer "the place" to be seen and you could shoot a cannon off inside and not hit anybody. The next month it's sold, the name is changed, and it's mobbed again.

The clientele in a typical nightclub is in the twenty-one- to thirty-five-year-old age group. The people who work in nightclubs, like the clientele, tend to be party lovers who travel in the fast lane. Many nightclubs are an integral part of the drug culture in today's society.

A nightclub will stay open as late as the law allows, with few daytime hours or none at all. As a nightclub bartender you will get out of work at 3:00 or 4:00 A.M., get to bed at 5:00, crawl out of bed at 2:00 P.M. and go back to work again at 7:00. Eventually you will become accustomed to these hours, forget what sunlight feels like, and start to enjoy living like a vampire.

Nightclubs have dancing, either with a DJ or live music, and most do not serve food. They do, however, serve a *lot* of alcohol. These are the places where you make all those exotic drinks. Because the pace here is fast, the fastest, most stylish, and most knowledgeable bartenders can be found in the popular nightclubs. Loud music and horrendous crowd noise force the nightclub bartender to develop a special skill—the ability to read lips.

The amount of alcohol you sell will relate directly to the amount of money you can earn in tips, so a fast-paced nightclub bar will provide an excellent income if you can handle the pressure and the hectic working conditions. You'll work hard and late, you'll be bombarded by loud music, you'll party after work until sunrise, then sleep all day. Is this fun? You bet it is—when you're young.

THE HOTEL BAR

The clientele in a hotel bar or lounge will vary depending on the style and location of the hotel. In or near a large city the clientele of a major hotel lounge will consist of traveling business people, tourists, and some local regulars.

Business people on expense accounts are generally the best tippers of all because they are used to dining out and are usually spending the company's money. They invariably use credit cards, which means that a line on the slip will be clearly marked "Tips," so they can't "forget." Also, business travelers often entertain clients, so they might kick in a little more than they normally would.

Most tourists are also likely to be free with the tips. Some tourists, however, come from countries where tipping is not customary, so they may leave no tip at all.

Bartending in a large hotel has several advantages over bartending in a small drinking establishment. Usually the hourly pay is higher; it may be very high, if the hotel is unionized. There is more job security in a large hotel because the management has to be careful about working conditions and conditions under which employees are fired. This is due to the power of the union, and if a particular hotel is not a union shop, management will still be careful because they're scared silly about a union coming in.

A large hotel will also offer group health insurance, a credit union, vacation pay, and discounts to full-time employees. There is also more opportunity for a bartender to move into management, if he takes leave of his senses, or to be transferred to another part of the country where the hotel has another property.

Since the money and conditions are so good in the large hotel lounges, there is less employee turnover. This means that there are more career bartenders in hotels than anywhere else, so it is more difficult to break in. A good time to try is just before or right after a new hotel opens. If you can break in, a lounge in a large, well-run hotel is an excellent place to tend bar.

THE COLLEGE BAR

Bars patronized primarily by college students are found near almost every campus in the country.

A college bar is a good place to obtain bartending experience because the management will be less particular about hiring trained, experienced bartenders. The compensation will not be as good in a typical college bar, however, as in other drinking establishments. Students are notoriously bad tippers, partly because they are young and naive to the ways of the world, and partly because they are always short of money. What kind of tip do you think you'll get from a poverty-stricken student who dumps a handful of nickels and dimes on the bar and says, "Is this enough for a draft beer?"

While you're in school, working in a college bar can be

a fun part-time job, a great way to meet people, and a good way to obtain valuable experience, but it is one hard way to make a living.

The Restaurant Bar

Many restaurants have full bars that attract a broad range of clients, from business people and tourists to families.

In many restaurant bars the bartender will serve an abridged menu, or even the full menu, at the bar. This can be an advantage when it comes to tip income because the total bill per customer will be much higher. Serving the full menu at the bar may complicate the bartender's job and slow down the customer turnover, but the net gain in tips will make up for these drawbacks. It's a simple formula: more service equals higher tips.

The typical restaurant bar serves lunch, which means there will be more work hours available for bartenders during the day. A full-time day position with a decent income may even be available—a rarity in the bartending business.

Most restaurant bars close earlier than nightclubs. This means there are fewer night hours available, but it also means that restaurant bartenders get off work in time to catch last call somewhere else. This is either an advantage or a disadvantage, depending on how you look at it.

Many restaurants have a service bar instead of a full bar. A service bar is a small, compact drink station with a pick-up area for the waiters but no stools for the customers. The service bartender simply makes the drinks, and the waiters pick them up and deliver them to the customers. The service bartender receives a salary plus a percentage of the waiters' tips, the theory being that a percentage of what the customer leaves as a tip is for the alcohol portion of the bill. The industry standard for tips to a service bartender is 10 percent. In other words, if a particular waiter makes ninety dollars one evening, at the end of the night he'll throw the service bartender nine dollars. And if he wants a little faster service, he might throw in a few bucks more. Service bartenders remember who is generous and who isn't. See how it works?

In a busy restaurant a service bartender will crank all night, which means he'll make drinks nonstop for the entire shift. With no customers to deal with—just a line of impatient waiters—the service bartender gets to know all the drink recipes and learns how to make the drinks quickly and in the most efficient order. Therefore, service bartending is a good training ground.

THE PRIVATE CLUB

Country clubs, yacht clubs, alumni clubs, and most other private clubs employ bartenders. Tending bar in a private club, however, will be somewhat different from working in a drinking establishment that's open to the general public.

Private clubs do not operate on the profit motive like regular establishments. They are usually run by a board of governors of some sort, made up of club members. This means that management does not operate within the constraints of bottom-line economics—or even within the bounds of common sense. Some of the wackiest management types in the world can be found in private clubs.

Bartenders in private clubs are paid at a higher than average hourly rate, but the practice of accepting tips is discouraged—although members and guests will occasionally slip you a five-spot. Members pay for their drinks by signing the bill onto a personal account, so there may be no cash transactions at all. The variety of drinks served will not be as great as in a nightclub, either—in other words, you will mix more martinis and manhattans than Fuzzy Navels and Orgasms.

Naturally, the clientele in a private club bar will consist of the same people over and over, and the bartender must relate well, not in order to make tips but just to keep her job. Also, you might have to give the members more freedom than you would allow customers in a regular bar. This means you can't shut them off as soon or throw them out as fast. After all, it's their club.

THE BANQUET BAR

Many caterers, hotels, and banquet halls employ bartenders on a full- or part-time basis. This type of job entails working behind a temporary or movable bar at parties and other social functions, although some banquet halls do have permanent bar setups.

Banquet bartenders generally receive a higher hourly rate than other bartenders, but they may not receive tips. Because of the limited setup, bartending at social functions is relatively uncomplicated and requires little experience. You may stock up to ten different types of liquor; five or six different juices, sodas, and mixers; a couple brands of bottled beer; red, white and rosé wine; and not much else.

If it is a cash bar, you will have a cash drawer and there will be only two or three price categories. Management will check up on you later by comparing the amount of liquor, the number of beer bottles, and the amount of wine you had when you started with the amount you finished with and reconciling this with the money in the cash drawer. (Liquor in bottles is measured by eye, estimated to the tenth.) If it isn't a cash bar, this same counting technique will be used to bill the person who is paying for the function.

Banquet bartending is ideal for part-time employment because the hours per shift are usually relatively short. The work may not be regular, however, because of seasonal fluctuations inherent in the banquet business—the wedding season, the graduation season, the holiday party season, and so on.

During a function, the banquet bartender stands behind a little bar on wheels and watches as the guests at the party interact, dance, talk business, give and receive awards, and make speeches. Every now and then a guest comes over, orders a couple of drinks and walks away. At some functions they may all line up at once, get their drinks, and then walk away. Either way, the bartender will not be a part of the action, as in a regular bar.

If part of the reason you want to tend bar is to be where the action is, or maybe even in the center of the action, banquet bartending is not for you. If you want to meet and talk to interesting people, banquet bartending is not for you. But if you just want to get in, get out, and put a few bucks in your pocket, by all means go down to the nearest Marriott Hotel or Holiday Inn and apply for a bartending job in the banquet division.

NINE

LANDING A BARTENDING JOB

The business of selling alcoholic beverages flourishes in this country and around the world. In poor economic times the bars are full of people drowning their sorrows. In boom times the bars are packed with people living it up and celebrating. Good bartenders are in demand everywhere.

Bartending is lucrative. In some establishments there is a great deal of money to be made—in cash. Bartending at night or on weekends is an ideal part-time job, if that's what you're after. As a bartender you'll meet and work with interesting people in a relaxed, enjoyable setting. Bottom line: bartending is fun.

Your first bartending job will be the most difficult to land. The owners and managers of drinking establishments will often state that they only want someone with experience. It is possible, however, to land a bartending job with no experience whatsoever if you follow this tried-and-true method.

The Seven-Step Approach to Getting a Job

Step 1

Read this manual thoroughly. Memorize all of the basic drink recipes and as many other recipes as possible. To simplify this monumental task of memorization, make flash cards with the drink names on the front and the ingredients on the back and have someone quiz you. Make sure you know the basic drinks cold.

Step 2

Decide which type of establishment you would prefer to work in. Do not be too picky, however. Your goal is to land any decent bartending job. Once you have obtained some experience, it will be much easier for you to switch to another type of establishment.

Step 3

Decide on the geographic area you would like to work in. Use a map. Be willing to travel, if necessary, to get to your first job.

Step 4

Write down the name, address, and telephone number of every drinking establishment in the geographic area you have chosen. In order to accomplish this, you may have to explore the area by car or on foot. In some localities it is possible to obtain from the town hall a list of all the pouring licenses that have been issued in that area. Write everything down and keep it in a file folder.

Step 5

Develop the right mental attitude before approaching any establishment. You must overcome your lack of confidence and outright fear. Do this by remembering five important facts:

1. Some managers and owners want to hire bartenders with no experience so they can train them their own way. In their view, "no experience" means "no bad habits."
2. Personal appearance and neatness along with a nice smile and a friendly manner are as important as prior experience when you're being interviewed for a bartending job.
3. You will have to talk to many owners and managers before you will find one who will hire you. Therefore, each one who doesn't hire you brings you one step closer to the one who will.
4. There is a steady turnover of employees in the bar business, and there are always job openings—if not right now, soon.
5. When you do get behind a bar you definitely will be able to perform well. By studying this manual alone you will be more knowledgeable than most bartenders in the field. There is always on-the-job training, too. All managers and owners expect all new bartenders to need a breaking-in period.

Step 6

Visit each of the establishments on your list. Now that you know what kind of bar you want to work in, you know where you want it to be, and you have the right attitude, you must systematically approach the task of getting hired.

This is the hardest step in the whole process. It may look easy on paper, but when it comes time to do it, Mount Everest seems to be looming up in front of you. Make up your mind, swallow your pride, stop worrying about making a fool out of yourself, develop a plan, and *do it!*

Plan to visit three or four establishments a day. The best time to apply for a job is between 10:00 and 11:00 A.M. or between 2:00 and 4:00 P.M. Do not apply during the busy hours or very late at night. Do not apply while you're sitting at the bar drinking tequila. Do not attempt to make friends with the bartender and apply that way; it won't work.

Walk in to the establishment and ask the first employee you see if the manager is available. When you meet the manager, *smile* and explain that you'd like to apply for a bartending job. If there are no openings, ask if you can fill out an application. Most managers will agree to this—if only to get rid of you.

Most job application forms are pretty much alike, with spaces for past employment, education, and so forth. You should have with you a small notepad with the dates of all past employment and education. This saves a lot of time. You won't have to sit around for half an hour scratching your head trying to remember what year you graduated from high school.

Make sure you get the manager's name before you leave. If the manager is not available, leave your application with an employee. To ensure that the form will reach the manager, ask the employee's name and the name of the manager, and jot both names down while the employee is watching.

Do not worry that you have no bartending experience to put down on the application. Your best chance of being hired comes during face-to-face contact with the manager. Remember the old saying: you only have one chance to make a first impression. *Smile,* dress neatly, and be friendly but businesslike.

Step 7

Follow up on your applications. If Step 6 was the hardest step, this step is the most important. Most of the time you will not get to speak to a manager on the first visit.

Call back as many times as you have to in order to speak directly to the manager. Again, do not call during the busy hours. If the manager is not available, and you failed to get her name during your visit, ask the person on the phone what the manager's name is, and then the next time you call you can ask for her by name. The bar business is a first-name business. Ask for the manager by her first name and you will usually get right through.

It is even more effective to follow up on an application in person. Your goal is to put a voice, face, and personality behind your application to make it stand out from the rest.

Write down the dates of each call and each contact with a manager, and keep this information on file. By contacting the manager once over the telephone, by dropping in during a slow hour to see if anything has opened up, and by putting a voice, face, and personality (hopefully sparkling) behind your application, you can help the manager forget that you have no bartending experience.

By being organized and contacting every manager of every drinking establishment on your list you will greatly increase the odds that you will be in the right place at the right time. Think of yourself as a farmer out in the fields planting seeds. Eventually some of these seeds will take root and grow. Keep in contact, keep coming around, and eventually you will be in position to harvest that job opening.

Record keeping is important. Your records will come in handy later when you want to switch to that fast-paced, high-paying job in the nightclub closer to your home. Imagine your telephone conversation to the manager of that nightclub: "Hello, Tom, this is Bill Smith. I've been bartending at Rick's Café for the past six months. It's nice there, but your place is a real first-class establishment and it's a lot closer to where I live. Are there any openings yet? . . . Oh, yeah? Great! I'll stop by tomorrow afternoon."

Your goal is to get a manager to grant you an interview. Do not make the mistake of giving up too soon. Within several weeks to several months you should have a job interview lined up. Looking for a bartending job is like being in sales when the product you are selling is yourself. If you work at it diligently for a little while, you'll soon get out of sales and into bartending, which is a lot easier. The secret is to have your application—backed up by a face, voice and personality—sitting on the manager's desk before an ad goes into the newspaper.

What do you say when you do get an interview? Well, the manager will already know that you do not have bartending experience because she has your application. What is she looking for? Somebody with a neat appearance who is a fast learner. Somebody who is dependable and will show up on time and never call in sick. Somebody who has confidence and good interpersonal skills—in other words, somebody who can handle himself and others. She also wants somebody who is very flexible about work hours. Figure out how to emphasize these qualities about yourself, and you're in.

So that's the seven-step approach. It's not easy. It requires diligence and guts, but it has worked for me on more than one occasion, and it can work for you, too. When you do get your first bartending job, you make it through those scary first few weeks, and you come home at the end of the night with a pocketful of cash, you'll look back and think it was a piece of cake.

The seven-step approach is one way to land your first job with no experience. Several lengthier or more costly paths are also available. Read on.

BARTENDING SCHOOL

Bartending courses are advertised in newspapers and the Yellow Pages. The best schools have a realistic bar setup and a cocktail lounge atmosphere. Look for a school that offers a lot of drink-making practice rather than lecturing. (Drinks are made using real liquor bottles filled with colored water.)

At a good school you will learn more drink recipes than you'll ever really need, and you will have them down cold, which is very important.

Many schools offer free job placement for their graduates. You should do some checking, however, to see if it is a successful program. Some schools have a reputation for turning out graduates with no useful knowledge and bad bartending habits. Bar managers in the community may have had bad experiences with graduates of certain schools. If you tell them you went there, they may laugh in your face and show you the door.

Other schools have very good reputations. Some bar managers will call the placement offices of good schools when they need to hire a bartender. Caterers and banquet facilities are known for going directly to schools for bartenders.

The disadvantages of attending bartending school is that it can cost several hundred dollars or more. It also takes time—usually forty to fifty hours spread over several weeks. However, if you do have the time and the money, it is a good idea to take one of the well-recognized courses. It gives you something to put down on your job application, it lets you get the feel of being behind a bar, and it's fun.

WORKING YOUR WAY UP

Another route to becoming a bartender is to start in a lower position, pay your dues, and work your way up. This means taking a job as a bar-back for a while until you gradually learn to tend bar.

A bar-back does all the dirty work behind the bar: setting up, filling ice bins, stocking and washing glasses, changing kegs, stocking bottled beer, filling juice containers, emptying bus buckets, breaking down, and mopping.

Bar-backing is a relatively low-paying unskilled job. You get an hourly rate plus a cut of the tips from the bartenders, usually a quarter to a half of what they make. This kind of job can be found in the want ads or by applying from bar to bar. Only a very busy establishment will hire a bar-back, though. In most establishments the bartenders themselves perform all these duties.

Before you take a position as a bar-back, make sure it is the policy of management to promote bar-backs to bartenders. Otherwise you might bust your rear end for six months lugging ice and kegs of beer around and then stand by while they hire a new bartender off the street.

On the other hand, some establishments insist that a person work as a bar-back before becoming a full-fledged bartender.

THE WANT ADS

It is difficult for a bartender with no experience to land a job through a want ad, because ads attract experienced bartenders who are looking to change jobs. Bartending jobs are in great demand, so there will be a lot of applications. Management has to eliminate applications from this pile. Guess which applications get tossed first?

Now you see the beauty of the seven-step approach, which gets you in there before an ad goes in the paper and puts a voice, face, and personality behind your application. By calling back and staying in regular contact with the managers, you relieve them of the need to advertise when a position opens up. *Capisce*?

Nevertheless, you should apply for every bartending job you see advertised in the paper, even if the ad specifies experienced bartenders only. You never know what might happen. Maybe the manager is from your hometown or went to the same school you did. Once in a while you will see an ad for a new hotel or large chain restaurant inviting people to apply for all positions. This is an excellent opportunity for a beginning bartender. Remember, dress neatly and smile when you apply for any job.

Friends and Relatives

If you have friends in the business, ask them to help you get a job. Managers or owners of drinking establishments will sometimes take the word of a trusted employee who recommends you. You'd better not screw up, though, once you get in there.

Do you have an uncle in the business? If all else fails, or maybe even before you try all else, go the nepotism route. Hit your uncle up for a job. You don't need me to tell you this, do you?

Landing a Bartending Job After You Have Experience

You have much to gain by becoming a bartender. You can make a decent living in any economic climate, no small advantage in itself. You can actually have fun while you are earning a living, and you can find a job anytime and anywhere you want.

You can land a bartending job without experience by using the seven-step approach, of course, but once you have experience in the business, your job search will become a lot easier.

Obviously, experience makes your application more attractive to managers. It allows you to compete for jobs advertised in the newspaper. What experience really does for you, though, is give you a feel for the business and a certain confidence that will be very apparent in a job interview. Once you have experience, the seven-step approach will work with incredible efficiency.

TEN

ONCE YOU STEP BEHIND THE BAR

Bartending is more than a job; it is a skilled trade that takes time and effort to learn. It is different from other trades in that a large portion of your pay is made up of tips from customers. Think of yourself as a subcontractor, a business within a business. Your business—what you have to trade— is knowledge and service. The better you perform your business, the more tips you will receive.

The success of your bartending business will depend on your *knowledge, style, speed,* and *etiquette.*

KNOWLEDGE

As a professional bartender you should be knowledgeable about liquors, liqueurs, wine, beer, and all ingredients used to make cocktails. You should know all popular drink recipes, and many less popular recipes, and you should know them so well that they are second nature to you. To acquire and maintain this knowledge, you should study, review, and keep up with new trends in the industry.

A professional bartender must be knowledgeable about current events, also. Take the time to read the newspaper every day. Know about business, sports, politics, the weather, movies, television, the horoscope, Ann Landers, and the latest lottery drawings. Subscribe to and read other popular periodicals. Become knowledgeable on a wide range of subjects and develop the ability to converse with your customers on these topics. This ability is an important part of the service you provide as a professional bartender, and it will greatly enhance your tip income. People expect bartenders to know a little about everything.

STYLE

Working behind a bar is a lot like being onstage. Many times you will find that customers are looking at you, watching your every move. It is to your benefit to develop a unique style behind the bar. All else equal, the bartender with the better style will get better tips. A number of elements, when combined, will create your style behind the bar.

Looking Good

Always maintain good posture behind the bar. Stand erect; do not slouch or lean on the bar when you take drink orders. When you're not busy, you may be tempted to drape yourself over the cash register or sit down on the beer chest. *Resist that urge.* Also, avoid touching your face or running your fingers through your hair. Customers notice these habits, if only on a subliminal level, and they will reduce your tip income. Don't smoke cigarettes behind the bar. It looks bad, and ashes might fall into the ice. Don't blow your nose or clean your ears or floss your teeth, either.

Make sure your uniform is clean at all times, and pay special attention to your hands and fingernails, especially if you have a second job during the day fixing automobile transmissions. If you wear your hair long, keep it tied back. If you want to grow a beard or mustache, do it during your vacation.

Paying Attention

Remain alert to your customers. Keep your head up and make eye contact. Do not watch TV or read while there are customers at the bar. Nothing is more annoying to a customer than to be in need of service while the bartender is glued to the playoff game on TV or engrossed in the crossword puzzle.

Keep your attention on *all* your customers. Don't get so engrossed in conversation with one that you ignore the others. If a customer is bending your ear and you have difficulty breaking away when someone else is flagging you down, just say, "Excuse me," and go take care of the other person. Those ear-bender types are used to people walking away in the middle of a sentence anyway. It drives customers crazy when they need something and the bartender is shooting the breeze with a co-worker or even another customer. It's the "Hey, what about me?" syndrome.

This brings us to what I call customer time, which is five times longer than actual time. In other words, one minute of actual time equals five minutes in customer time. For example, let's say a customer walks up to the bar. The bartender is way down at the other end discussing yesterday's football game with his favorite customer. While the new customer looks at the taps and dreams about the ice-cold beer he plans to order, one minute of actual standard time goes by. The customer starts tapping his fingers on the bar, waiting. Another minute of actual time goes by. Finally the bartender strolls down and greets the new customer, who seems a little surly. The bartender doesn't understand why. After all, it was only a couple minutes, right?

Wrong. Those two minutes you spent playing Monday morning quarterback equaled ten minutes in customer time. And ten minutes is a long time to wait.

If the bar is not too busy, you should give people a few seconds before asking them what they want. Wait until they are settled before you greet them. It is annoying to have a bartender jump all over you before you even get your rear end down on the stool. Believe it or not, some people didn't decide what they were going to order while they were in the car on the way over.

Being Cheerful and Friendly

Smile when you greet customers. This may be the most underused technique of all, but it is probably the most powerful in increasing tips. Part of your job as a professional bartender—strange as it may seem—is to be in a good mood. People do not come to a drinking establishment to interact with a crabby bartender. They don't care if you have personal problems or you just totaled your car or your dog just died. If you're not in a good mood, and just can't fake it, at least be "neutral." In other words, make it so that even in your worst possible mood you exhibit a robot-like courteousness. This takes a lot of practice, but it's a skill you must develop if you want to be a professional.

Get in the habit of using a friendly greeting like, "Hi. How are you? What can I start you off with today?" Do not point at the customer and say, "What do you want?" Do not shout, "Next!" and then stand there with an impatient look on you face. Does that sound unlikely? Observe bartenders in the field and you will be surprised at how many act as though they are doing you a favor by waiting on you. A cheerful smile and a friendly greeting can make the difference between an average tip and a great tip.

Starting Out Right

Wipe the bar surface in front of customers when they sit down, whether it needs it or not. This is a small step, but it has a subliminal effect, and many small steps add up to bigger tips. Place napkins or coasters on the bar while taking the order, and turn the napkin so the logo faces the customer. This should be automatic.

Pouring Properly

Start building a cocktail by filling the glass to the top with ice unless the customer specifically asks for less ice. A cocktail made with less ice will have more mixer and will taste and look weak.

Learn to pour liquor while holding the bottle straight up and down, whether you are free-pouring or measuring a shot. This takes a little practice, but it looks much more professional and stylish than if you hold the bottle in a horizontal position. Of course, some bottles—Amaretto and Chambord, for example—cannot be held straight up and down because they don't have a neck.

Mixing Drinks Stylishly

Practice a stylish way to shake cocktails. One way is to grasp the mixing glass with one hand and the shaker cup with the other, hold them together tightly, and shake first over one shoulder and then over the other. If your hand is big enough, grasp both together in one hand and shake. Make sure the mixing glass and metal cup are jammed together tightly, though, or you'll get an ice-cold margarita down your back! When you finish shaking, always place the combination back on the rail with the metal shaker cup on the bottom and the serving glass or mixing glass on top. Remove glass and pour *from* the metal cup *into* the glass. This will prevent spillage down the outside of the serving glass.

Garnishing and Serving

When you squeeze a lime as a garnish, always use one hand to cover the side nearest the customers. This will prevent juice from squirting in someone's eye, and more importantly, it looks stylish. It's one more of those tiny subliminal steps.

When you hand the cocktail to the customer or place it on the napkin in front of her, do not touch the rim of the glass with your fingers. Professional bartenders don't do that.

Clearing the Bar and Settling the Bill

Do not remove a customer's cocktail before asking if she is finished. If the glass is obviously empty, ask if she would like another drink before removing the old one. The object is to let your customers know you are aware of them, without making them feel rushed or pressured. Always use a fresh glass when you make a second cocktail.

Give customers back their change in an orderly fashion. All the bills should be facing the same way, and the coins should be grouped together, not scattered all over the bar.

Serving Customers Who Smoke

Keep a lighter in your pocket at all times as part of your uniform. When a customer reaches for a pack of cigarettes, whip your lighter out with a flourish and give her a light. A cigarette lighter will pay for itself a hundred times.

Keep all of the ashtrays clean. Ideally they should be emptied after only one cigarette has been stubbed out. This shows customers that you are really on the ball and has a great effect on tips. For that matter, keep a pack of cigarettes and a newspaper behind the bar at all times for the customers' convenience. You'll make the cost of those items back many times over in above-average tips.

Putting on a Show

Try to develop your own hotdog moves behind the bar. Perform for your customers, being careful not to overdo it. Some bartenders are able to pour liquor with the bottle several feet from the glass. Others can free-pour with two liquor bottles in either hand. Others toss the mixing equipment around like jugglers. Of course, your freedom to hotdog may be limited to the policy and style of the establishment you work in. Tom Cruise's character in the movie *Cocktail* must have worked for a very understanding owner; he kept the bottles flying around all over the place.

Watch other bartenders to pick up some tricks. Practice different hotdog moves as often as you can. The simple act of removing the cap from a beer bottle can be performed several different ways. With practice, you will be able to amaze your customers by lining up five beer bottles on the rail and opening them in astonishingly rapid succession, all the while tossing the caps over your shoulder into the garbage can without looking. This is fun for the customers, a mild diversion after a long day's work, and they won't mind leaving a bigger tip as a price for the entertainment.

It will take some time to develop style behind the bar. Some bartenders work for years and never even try to develop a unique style. Don't make this mistake. As soon as you step behind a bar start working on your style. Borrow and adapt other bartenders' moves. Then practice and practice some more, and eventually you will develop a style that customers will recognize. And unless that shaker cup slips out of your hand and that mai tai soars through the air and lands in somebody's lap, you'll be rewarded with bigger tips.

SPEED

Often the best money to be made bartending is in high-volume establishments. The more drinks you sell, the more tips you will make; it's as simple as that. It is very important to become as fast as possible behind the bar.

Knowledge

One of the keys to real speed is knowledge of drink recipes. (Notice that I keep stressing this.) You must know all drink recipes cold—so cold that they are automatic. In order to reach this point, you must *memorize* and *practice*. Use flash cards. Quiz yourself. Develop your own memory aids for the recipes. (Some are provided with the recipes in Chapters 12 and 13.) Real practice will come in a real-life situation. You will be amazed at how quickly you will learn drink recipes when you have to make them in a high-pressure situation behind the bar.

Physical Condition

Another important and often neglected factor that will affect your speed behind the bar is physical conditioning. In a high-volume establishment you will be on your feet and constantly moving, sometimes for seven or eight hours straight. You might be lugging cases of beer and buckets of ice around, or rearranging those unwieldy kegs. You will definitely be lifting and pouring from bottles constantly. Bartending in a busy establishment can be a physically taxing job. It is difficult to be fast when you are tired and aching. Here are some exercises you can do every day to keep yourself in condition:

> 25 push-ups, for moving kegs
> 25 sit-ups, for a flat stomach and a better appearance
> 25 deep-knee bends, for strong legs
> 25 arm-curls, for carrying cases of beer
> 10 minutes of jumping rope, for increased endurance
> 5 minutes of hand flexing, for hand strength

If you stick to this simple routine, which isn't easy, you will find that your work is less stressful and you have more energy. When you feel better you are more likely to be in a good mood and to smile more often and with more sincerity. That means you will make more tips.

Bar Layout

Knowing your bar layout is also very important for speed. You should strive to reach the point where you can find any bottle or piece of equipment with your eyes closed. This will allow you to develop identical moves—a vital element of speed behind the bar. It means that you will make a drink the same way each time. For example, you'll build a gin and tonic as follows: left hand reaches for highball glass while right hand reaches for ice scoop; glass is filled with ice and placed on rail with left hand while right hand reaches for gin bottle in speed rack; right hand pours gin in glass (bottle straight up and down) while left hand removes soda gun from holster; left hand operates soda gun and fills glass with tonic water while right hand takes lime wedge from garnish tray; left hand holsters soda gun, takes sip stick from holder, and inserts it into cocktail; right hand squeezes garnish while left hand shields customers from squirting juice; lime wedge is dropped in cocktail and cocktail is served to customer (not touching rim of glass with fingers). Elapsed time: eight seconds actual time, or forty seconds of customer time. No time is allotted for standing there scratching your head while you try to remember what goes into a gin and tonic.

If you perform the same motions each time you make a particular cocktail, and know your bar layout, you can concentrate on increasing your speed. Other movements may be involved, like taking three steps down the bar to get a particular liquor bottle. If so, practice every step. (Do you think Baryshnikov learned just a few parts of each ballet?) Eventually you will have repetitious moves for combinations of cocktails and complicated frozen drinks. You will be poetry in motion.

Grouping Drinks

Increase your speed even more by learning to group the drinks in your mind. Say you get an order for a gin and tonic, a glass of white wine, a sea breeze, a Budweiser draft, and a Dewar's on the rocks. Focus first on the mixed drinks by taking two highball glasses, filling them with ice at the same time, and placing them on the rail. Then fill a rocks glass with ice and place it on the rail. Pour gin and vodka in the two highball glasses at the same time. (This is a bar where you can free-pour, okay?) Pour the Dewar's into the rocks glass while you add tonic water to the gin. Pour grapefruit and cranberry juice over the vodka at the same time to make the sea breeze. Pour the wine and the beer last so the wine will be chilled and the beer will still have a head on it when you serve it. By grouping the drinks, from mixed drinks to wine to beer, you will remember the order more easily and have to make fewer movements, which will increase your speed.

Preparation

The most neglected key to speed behind the bar is adequate preparation. You must be stocked and ready for the rush when it comes. Your repetitious moves will come to a screeching halt if you empty a liquor bottle and there is no backup handy, or when you reach for the ice and there is none. Being prepared means having glasses stocked, ice bins filled, juice bottles filled, and backups handy for liquor bottles, soda boxes or canisters, beer kegs, and whatever else you need.

Preparation is what separates the really fast bartenders from the average bartenders. Keep preparing whenever you have a chance. When you get a lull in the action, do not just stand around resting. Refill the juice bottles, stock fresh glasses, or get more ice. This will enhance your speed by allowing you to work nonstop during the rush. It will also make your job easier and less stressful. You will become frustrated if you have to stop in the middle of a drink order, when the bar is three-deep with screaming customers, and make a new batch of sour mix because some bonehead you work with used the last of it and never made any more.

Always leave the mixing equipment in position and ready to use. This means rinsing out mixing glasses, shaker cups, strainers, bar spoons, and blender cups immediately after you use them and leaving them in the proper position on the drainboard. You or one of your co-workers will be thrown off the track if you reach for the shaker cup and it isn't there. You will be stopped dead in your tracks, your beautiful balletlike moves interrupted, if the vodka collins you make has a funny pink color because the bartender before you did not rinse out the mixing cup properly after making a Bloody Mary.

Know the Order

Learn to keep the drink orders straight. When you are working quickly, going flat out, nothing slows you down more than mistakes. You may be taking more orders than you can easily remember and thinking ahead to the next one while you are mixing cocktails. The fastest bartenders are able to take several drink orders, keep them all in order, and carry on a conversation with a customer while they mix the cocktails. This takes a lot of practice. One way to keep the drinks straight is to cement them in your mind by repeating the drinks as you place ice in each glass. Know your limits of memorization and try not to overextend yourself.

Time to Pay

Another important part of your job is operating the cash register. You must be as fast as possible on the cash register, but you must also be accurate. Making change for customers is obviously a crucial part of the entire transaction. You don't want to screw up here because the management in most establishments will expect the bartenders to make up any shortage between the cash register ring-out and what is actually in the drawer. In other words, if you come up short at the end of the night, you pay. If you end up with too much money, management keeps the overage and you just look bad. Funny how that works, isn't it?

To reduce the chance of giving a customer the wrong change, make a habit of repeating the denomination of the bill out loud when you take it from the customer. For example, as you take the bill from her hand, say "That will be seven-fifty . . . out of twenty." Say it clearly and hold the bill up for her and others to see as you take it. When you place it in the drawer, leave the clip up or, better yet, place the bill on top of the register or on the little shelf over the drawer until you have removed the proper change.

If you do forget what the denomination of the bill was, just ask the customer what she gave you. Most people will tell the truth when asked point-blank like this. If a customer claims that you shortchanged him, it is best not to argue unless you are absolutely certain.

You must develop good money-handling habits and procedures that you always follow. If there ever is a time when you might want to slow down and be deliberate, it is during the money-handling part of the transaction. You do not want to come up short at the end of the night and have to kick in some of your hard-earned tips and listen to those whining managers.

Mental Conditioning

Mental control is also important in increasing your speed. Sometimes the bar will be jammed and everything will be working beautifully. You and your crew will be operating like a well-oiled machine, making drinks amazingly fast, delighting the adoring customers with your flashy style. The tip jar is overflowing as people practically throw money at you.

There will be other nights when nothing goes right. In the middle of the rush you'll break a glass in the ice. Customers will be screaming at you as orders pile up. You'll make five frozen strawberry drinks for one party when they asked for banana. You'll run out of beer in the middle of the next order. To use an old bartending phrase, you are "in the weeds." When this happens, make a conscious effort to slow your frantic pace. Focus on one order or even one drink at a time, and block out all other distractions. Gradually build your speed back up, concentrating on identical moves. Remind yourself that the shift will eventually end, as all shifts do. Do not take your frustration out on your fellow bartenders. You guys are in this together. Picture yourself sitting down at the end of the night with a cold beer and a pile of tips. This thought alone will help you through many disastrous nights.

Don't Forget the Customer

Acknowledge your customers when you fall behind. When the bar is busy many customers will have to wait a while to order their drinks from you. They may even have to fight just to get noticed. If they have to wait too long, or if they feel that they are being intentionally ignored, they will feel justified in stiffing you. One way to avoid this is to keep your head up while bartending and make eye contact with customers, acknowledging their presence. Even if it takes a few minutes to get to them, at least they will know you are trying.

Let the customers know that there is method to your madness by saying something like "Sorry about the wait, I'll be right with you," or "You're on deck right after this gentleman here," or "Sir, what can I start you off with tonight?" It is amazing how many bartenders actually avoid eye contact when they are busy. This is unprofessional and very frustrating to customers. A frustrated customer is not a good tipper. A customer who appreciates how busy you are—and who sees the professional and fair manner in which you handle the throngs clamoring for drinks—is a good tipper.

A professional bartender thrives on volume. The more drinks he sells, the more money he makes. Therefore, the highest paying bartending jobs are in establishments where the bar is often crowded and the pace is extremely hectic. If you develop good speed habits and the right attitude, you will be able to handle this type of high-pressure job. Your rewards will include the admiration of the unskilled masses and cash in your pocket at the end of the shift.

ETIQUETTE

Bartending requires constant contact with the public in a social setting, complicated by the fact that the product you are selling has a powerful effect on people. The best long-range policy is to maintain a polite, professional attitude and keep your distance from your clientele. Professional etiquette demands that you avoid becoming too chummy with the customers. You must be friendly and cordial, of course, but it is not a good idea to socialize with customers outside of work. There's a subtle line here, but as a professional you should recognize it and not cross it. After all, does a psychiatrist party with his patients? Does the judge hang out with the defendant? Does the government official play golf with the defense contractor? Oh, well, you know what I mean.

Current Events

As I mentioned earlier, it is essential for the professional bartender to keep abreast of current events. Customers will often turn to you for conversation and opinion, and even to settle the occasional dispute. The bartender who is knowledgeable and a good conversationalist will make the most tips. Take care, however, to avoid heated conversations with customers on topics that might offend, like sex, politics, or religion. It may be fine with one particular customer, but the person sitting two seats down listening to you call a local politician a liar and a cheat, might be his campaign manager or, worse, his brother!

Avoid Gossip

Professional ettiquette also demands that you avoid talking about one customer to another. That is the height of unprofessional behavior. The clientele and atmosphere of many drinking establishments lend themselves to gossiping, but you must not gossip. Think of yourself as a human Switzerland. You are neutral. If someone asks you what you think of a particular fellow—while licking his lips in anticipation of juicy gossip—say, "He's not a bad guy," or "Fine human being, fine gentleman, never had a problem with him." If this is your response time and time again eventually the gossips will leave you alone, abandoning you as useless when it comes to uncovering dirt on someone. If you do engage in gossip, as sure as the sun rises in the east, your words will come back to haunt you. What goes around comes around, as they say. People love to gossip, but they respect someone who doesn't.

Ignore Poor Tippers

Another rule of ettiquette stipulates that you must never discuss the amount of a tip with a customer. If a customer leaves a poor tip for seemingly no reason, pick it up and thank him as if it were a normal tip. Do not say something like, "Gee, why are you leaving me such a lousy tip? Did I do something wrong?" You will be tempted to do this from time to time, especially if your service is good and it's a regular customer who undertips you all the time, or if you get completely stiffed on a large tab.

Let me explain why you should ignore poor tippers and outright stiffs. First of all, it's inappropriate and unprofessional to question customers about their tips. If you do question them, they have a perfect right to complain to a manager. Second, all you accomplish is to put yourself in a bad mood, which will make it more difficult to provide good service and get a good tip from the next customer. Third, you will learn with experience that tips average out at the end of the shift to about the same percentage of gross sales, no matter what you do. For every undertipper there is an overtipper, so it's just not worth it to get bogged down worrying about one ignorant stiff.

Examine the specific situation. Was your service lacking in any way? Be honest with yourself. If it was, then the stiff was doing you a favor by pointing this out. Correct the problem. If your service wasn't lacking, what can you do about it? There are stiffs out there, there always were, and there always will be. Shrug it off. If you have to wait on the same stiff every day, do it quickly and professionally. Get this customer out of the way fast so you can move on to the real tippers.

Getting Non-Tippers to Tip

Here are a few ways to encourage stiffs to cough up a decent tip. When you hand the change back to a customer who has stiffed you earlier, put the bills down on the bar, but keep the coins in your hand, which you hold out palm up. It takes a real hard-core stiff to take the nickels and dimes right out of your hand.

Here's another trick I call the dirty-bill routine. Find the dirtiest, most wrinkled, thin, worn out dollar bill you can. It's even better if it's torn or if it's been ripped in half and then taped together crookedly with hairy tape. When you give this bill as change, the customer will almost always leave it as a tip. Retrieve it out of the tip jar and give it as change again to someone else. Do this again and again. That's called making money work for you!

If you're lucky, one of the other customers at the bar will educate the stiff for you. Don't complain to other customers about the guy who just walked away and left you a dime on a nineteen-dollar drink order. Pick up the dime, look at it, turn it over, shake your head, and exclaim to yourself, loud enough for some customers to hear, "Gee, he must have been one of the Rockefellers." Put the dime in the tip jar and go on with your work.

Free Drinks

Almost every drinking establishment attracts a certain number of barflies and other assorted lowlifes who will try to befriend you in the hope that eventually you will start slipping them free drinks. They will say clever things like "Hey, this one is a tin roof special, right? On the house!"

How can you deal with these people without violating the rules of professional etiquette?

As a professional bartender make it a policy never to give away free liquor and never to overpour. When you give someone a free drink, the customer will probably leave you a larger than normal tip, but unless you own the place and it's your liquor to give away, this is outright stealing.

Unfortunately, however, some establishments have a policy where the bartender is allowed to give free drinks to customers who have been coming there for many years or who have spent a great deal on a given night. In my opinion, this is a stupid policy. Giving free drinks to people accomplishes two things. If there is a no-free-drink policy, it advertises to people that you are dishonest. It also attracts a clientele of freeloaders who come to expect those free cocktails. Freeloaders are like fleas; they aren't easy to get rid of once you have them.

Before your friends come to visit you in your place of employment, tell them not to expect any free drinks. If you want to buy somebody a drink, tell the manager or head bartender what you intend to do, take the money out of your pocket, ring the drink up on the register, put the money in the drawer, and keep the receipt. That is the way to do it. You may get away with slipping free drinks to friends for a while, but you'll eventually get caught. Being the big shot by providing free drinks does not outweigh the humiliation and economic setback of getting fired. Are your friends going to pay your bills while you're out there pounding the pavement, looking for a new job with no reference from your last one?

There are a few other things you will have to deal with

once you step behind the bar. Among them are spotters, shutting people off, dealing with the bartender mystique, serving couples, and carding.

SPOTTERS

Spotters—sometimes called shoppers, and sometimes called other things that I can't put into print—are spies hired by management to pose as customers, while watching your every move and evaluating your service. They will submit a report, which will usually start with an evaluation of the host or hostess and move on to the bartenders and other personnel. Spotters will pass judgement on every single aspect of the dining and drinking experience, and they will also provide their opinions and observations. They may report, for example, that "The bartender, a chubby male Caucasian with thick glasses and a receding hairline, was more interested in the basketball game on TV than in waiting on guests."

Not all establishments employ spotters, but if you work in one that does, you should treat all your customers as if they were spotters. There is nothing as humiliating and dehumanizing as finding yourself on the receiving end of a bad spotter's report. You feel like a character out of George Orwell's *1984*, being watched by Big Brother. You run the risk of losing your job because of a bad spotter's report, yet you never get to face your accuser, who always remains anonymous and may be lying.

Spotters are tricky, but there are a few ways to recognize them. Usually spotters are restaurant managers who do this type of spying on the side, or they are cop "wanna-bes," like mall security guards. They usually work in pairs, sometimes as a male and female couple. If you work in a full-service restaurant, they will usually stop at the bar for a cocktail and an appetizer and then move on to a table. They never have more than one or two cocktails. If the restaurant is not busy and there is no wait for a table, their modus operandi really stands out. They will ask a lot of stupid questions about the drinks or the menu in order to test your knowledge and your patience. They are looking for you to recommend things and do some ''up-selling,'' which means saying, ''Would you like Absolut vodka in that?'' when somebody orders a vodka and tonic, for example.

Spotters will watch very closely while you make cocktails to see if you are overpouring. They will watch very closely while you make cash transactions—or go anywhere near the cash register, for that matter. Spotters will always take the receipt with them when they leave the bar, not only to make sure it is correct, but to give it to their employer so they can be reimbursed.

If you work in a place that utilizes spotters, and you have a man and a woman sitting at the bar who look like restaurant-manager types or security guards, who are not interacting like a normal couple, who ask a lot of dumb questions about the menu or drink specials, who watch you like hawks, who have one drink and one appetizer each, and who take the receipt with them and move on to a table when there was no wait for a table in the first place, then chances are Big Brother is watching you. Send the word out to the wait staff that there may be spotters in the house. Write down on a piece of paper the time, the date, what they looked like, and what they drank and ate. Call the manager over and say, ''You know, when we get a bad spotter's report we can get fired, right? If that's the case, shouldn't we get a raise when we get a good spotter's report?''

SHUTTING PEOPLE OFF

The time will come when you, as a professional bartender, will have to shut someone off—refuse to serve him any more alcohol. This can occur when a customer is drunk and unruly and is disturbing other customers. It may also happen when a customer becomes a liability. In many states the bartender, as well as the owner of the establishment, can be held legally responsible if a patron is involved in an automobile accident or any other kind of accident after leaving a drinking establishment. Because of the increased awareness of drunk driving in today's society, the penalties have become much more severe. An establishment can lose a lawsuit and sometimes its liquor license, which will force it out of business. Gone are the days when you could serve 'em until they fell off the stools.

I'd like to say that it's a simple cut-and-dried task to shut somebody off, but it isn't. No matter how you phrase your request, you're saying to the customer, "You are unable to judge for yourself how much alcohol you can handle, so I have to make that decision for you." This is not an easy thing to say to somebody, whether he is younger or older than you, a stranger or a longtime customer, a bum or a pillar of society. Unfortunately, in drinking establishments as well as in other parts of our society, individual responsibility seems to be a thing of the past.

Of course, it's not that difficult to refuse somebody alcohol when he staggers up to the bar reeking of gin, unable to focus his eyes, slams his fist down and yells, "Yo, buddy, gimme a shota whiskey 'n' a beer!" Usually, however, it's a much more subtle situation.

How do you know when somebody is over the limit? And what is the limit, anyway? It may be different in the corner pub or private club than it is in the family restaurant. This is the first thing the bartender has to determine: how drunk are the customers allowed to get? You have to set a consistent tone for your establishment that doesn't vary from night to night.

Different people handle alcohol differently. It's partly a matter of metabolism. A 300-pound man can consume more alcohol to less effect than a 120-pound woman. It's also partly a matter of practice. An experienced drinker will show less outward effect to the same amount of alcohol as an inexperienced drinker, even though their blood alcohol content is exactly the same. Rate of consumption is important, too, and outside factors might be involved—fatigue, for example, or the amount of food consumed, or drugs taken in combination with alcohol. It takes experience and an understanding of human nature to shut people off in an effective and professional manner.

Let's say for argument's sake that you tend bar in a restaurant where the lunch crowd is made up mostly of business people and the evening rush consists of couples, families, and tourists who order drinks and dinner. There is a nice relaxed atmosphere at the bar where people can enjoy pleasant conversation along with their cocktails after work or while they wait for their table. In other words, people don't come to your bar to do shots of tequila, sing songs, get loaded, and pick fights.

Now let's say a middle-aged man is sitting at this bar. He's about five-ten, 170 pounds, wearing a business suit. You don't know his name, but he's been in before—you think he might work in the neighborhood—and he's always been pleasant. He's been there about an hour, and in that time you've served him four vodka and sodas. He's not eating anything, and by observing closely you detect the signs of drunkenness. His eyes are red, and he's laughing a little too loud at the news on TV, which isn't even funny. He lights the wrong end of a cigarette while he's already got one burning in the ashtray. You begin to suspect that he may have had a few cocktails in the bar next door before he came in. You offer him an appetizer menu, but he waves it away. He finished the last two cocktails more quickly than the first two, and now he's starting to butt in on the conversation going on next to him. You try to slow the pace of his drinking by not asking him if he wants another one when his glass is empty. You hope he'll ask for the bill, but instead he holds up his empty glass and beckons you over. You decide to shut him off. Here's what you do: Inform the manager right away that you intend to shut off this customer. (This is the only real service that a manager can perform—backing you up in a situation like this.) Then inform the other bartenders. Approach the customer, who will now slide his empty glass toward you. An exchange similar to the following should now take place:

CUSTOMER:
I'll have another one a these here.

BARTENDER:
I'm sorry, sir. I can't serve you any more alcohol. Would you like some coffee instead?

CUSTOMER:
What? Coffee? Come on, pal, don't yank my chain. It's okay. Gimme one last drink.

BARTENDER:
(*Shaking his head*) Can't do it, sir.

CUSTOMER:
Just give me one last drink, will ya? I'm not driving.

BARTENDER:
Blame it on the lawyers, sir. Unfortunately we're liable in this type of situation, and we could lose our license. Would you like to talk to a manager?

CUSTOMER:
Oh, hell!

BARTENDER:
If we could just settle this tab we'll be all set, unless you would like something nonalcoholic.

CUSTOMER:
I come inna this joint all the time, you know.

BARTENDER:
I know. I've seen you before, and I hope we see you again, too. Thank you. I can take this whenever you're ready. (*Leaves the tab and walks away.*)

The key phrase to remember is "polite but firm." Lean on the bar and get as close to the customer as possible. Look him directly in the eye and speak quietly, so that others around will not hear you. Most customers will accept your decision with no argument, wishing to avoid an embarrassing scene. A few will argue a little, but if you stick to your guns, you will have no problem. A few will argue and get violent, or yell and create a scene. Do not back down. Be like the baseball umpire: never change your mind, no matter what. Never, never reverse your position and give the customer another drink. Call the police if you have to. Forget about humiliating or offending drunken customers—they have already embarrassed themselves. Ignore their threats to retaliate, or to call the owner of the establishment. Most people who have been shut off will realize the next day that you did them a favor. Many won't even remember what happened. One thing is for sure: you won't see them again for a while.

If you set a consistent level at which you and all the other bartenders in your establishment shut people off, eventually you will have a reputation, and problems will be few and far between. Customers will sense when they are approaching this level and they will shut themselves off. Then they will go down the street to the bar where the bartenders *never* shut anybody off, and they'll drink until they pass out, but at least you won't have to deal with the trouble they might cause.

THE BARTENDER MYSTIQUE

Now on to a more pleasant subject—what is sometimes called the bartender mystique. This is an aura that surrounds bartenders and somehow makes them attractive to the opposite sex. This goes for both male and female bartenders, although this effect is more obvious with female bartenders because most customers at bars are males.

An attractive female bartender is often in a precarious position because the job requires her to be friendly and outgoing. Certain men, unfortunately, interpret any woman's friendliness as a come-on. Misunderstandings are inevitable, mainly because some losers want to believe they have a chance when in fact absolutely no chance exists. A bartender should adopt a policy of *never* going out with customers. Once she earns the respect of her customers and sets the boundaries, a female bartender is in a position to earn a lot of money, simply because most male bar customers will leave bigger than average tips for a female bartender who knows how to handle them. In other words, men appreciate being handled well.

Eventually the regular male clientele will adopt a protective big-brother attitude toward the female bartender and will serve as a security force should any outsider decide to harass her. It goes without saying that a male bartender should not allow customers to make sexual comments or harass his female co-worker in any way, and he should not offer to get a male customer a date with his female co-worker.

As a male bartender, you will notice that women sitting at the bar often seem to be attracted to you. This is the bartender mystique at work. An attractive woman sitting at a bar alone, or even with friends, is often approached by men trying to pick her up. When these clowns start to annoy her, she looks to the bartender as a protector, somebody with whom she can occupy herself until they go away, or somebody who can make the men leave her alone. At the same time, you are serving her alcohol, which is lowering her inhibitions. A bond of friendship can develop between you, sometimes very quickly. You need to remember that if you were on the other side of the bar trying to pick her up, she would have nothing to do with you. She trusts you because you have a legitimate reason to be there; it's your job. You may be tempted to take advantage of the situation, but as a professional bartender you must not exploit your position; you will be better off in the long run.

All right, perhaps the man or woman of your dreams is sitting right there at your bar. You gaze into this customer's eyes and realize at that instant that you have found your lifetime mate. If that's the case, by all means call the phone number that he or she scribbled on a beverage napkin and pressed into your hand. Sacrifice your professionalism if you're absolutely certain that this is the real thing.

Serving Couples

In most drinking establishments you will have as part of your clientele at the bar couples, that is men and women sitting together who are either married or dating. If you are a male bartender, be careful not to focus all your attention on the female, no matter how attractive she is. This is annoying for the man with her. The same goes in reverse for a female bartender; don't spend a disproportionate amount of your service on the man. Make a concerted effort to divide your eye contact equally. People are very intuitive and alert to body language. They will recognize when a bartender is flirting with their spouse or their date, and most will not take kindly to it. Then again, they may be swingers and want to invite you over for a threesome. Be professional, will you? Do not socialize with your clientele!

Carding

There will be times behind the bar when it will be necessary to card your customers—that is, to ask for their identification cards in order to check their ages. Many states have become very strict about preventing minors from purchasing alcohol. Many cities and towns conduct sting operations in which undercover police officers accompanied by minors attempt to purchase alcoholic beverages in local drinking establishments. The penalties for serving a minor include stiff fines and suspension or loss of license. If you have any doubt at all whether a customer is old enough to purchase alcohol—twenty-one in all states—ask for ID.

Do not worry about offending someone by asking for ID. First of all, it's your job. Secondly, customers who look young will be used to it. Ironically, the people who moan and groan the most about being carded are usually about twenty-two years old. A good way to put a customer, especially a woman, in a good mood is to ask for her ID when you know she is old enough. Ask a couple in their seventies if you can see their IDs and you will always get a smile. And that is what you want—smiles. Happy clients, after all, are likely to be generous tippers.

Most states require a picture ID as proof of age, either a driver's license or a special liquor ID card. A passport is also acceptable. When you are handed the ID, take a close look at the picture to make sure it matches up with the person who gave it to you. Skin color, hairstyle, facial hair, and even eye color are changeable. Look at the nose. If the nose in the picture does not look like the nose on the person in front of you, you may have a fake ID. Now look at the date of birth. Has it been tampered with? Is the person who gave you the ID acting nervous?

If you have any doubt at all about the authenticity of the card, give the person a little quiz. Smile and say, "When were you born?" You'll be amazed at how many people who use a fake ID—or borrow an ID from a friend or relative who looks a little like them—neglect to memorize their new birth date. You can also ask them to tell you their Social Security number if you're in a state where it doubles as your license number. If they goof it up, you have a fake ID on your hands. You can either confiscate it and call the police or give it back along with a lecture about obeying the law. Watch out for other people trying to order for the minor, and if you work in a restaurant, watch out for the minor trying to order again once he or she gets to a table.

Every profession has an etiquette and a code of ethics, and bartending is no different. Like any other element of bartending, etiquette must be learned and practiced until it becomes second nature. If you develop proper etiquette and stick with it, in the long run your job will be easier and you will earn more money. Isn't that what we all want?

ELEVEN

ABOVE AND BEYOND

It is in your best interest as a professional bartender to build up a steady, reliable clientele of pleasant, nonviolent people who are also, hopefully, good tippers. Unless you work in some remote outpost, however, chances are your bar won't be the only drinking establishment in town. You will be in fierce competition with other places for customers' disposable income. Where do people want to go for a cocktail? Into whose eager palm do they want to place their tips? Would you like it to be yours? Here are a few ways to make your service stand out above and beyond the rest.

THE NAME GAME

Somebody once said there is no sweeter sound on earth than the sound of one's own name. As a professional bartender you should learn your customers' names and use them. Make a practice of writing down names to cement them in your mind. If somebody gives you a credit card, look at the name and then, when you give the card back, say, "Thank you, Mr. So-and-So." In this situation your younger clients often ask you to call them by their first name. Take them seriously: if a customer says, "Please call me James," don't address him as Jimbo or Jimmy-baby. The fact of the matter is, people have been watching *Cheers* reruns for so long they really do want to go "where everybody knows your name."

READING THE CUSTOMER

Just like a great quarterback can drop back into the pocket and read the defense in a matter of seconds, so should a great bartender be able to read the customers. For example, if a man wearing a bow tie comes into the bar every afternoon at precisely the same time, sits in exactly the same seat, places exactly the same orders, leafs quickly and efficiently through the *Wall Street Journal*, never talks to anybody, leaves a 15 percent tip, and never stays longer than twenty minutes, you can safely assume that he is not the one on whom to try out your newest shaggy dog joke.

Usually the situation is more subtle than that. Look carefully at your customers and size them up. Do they want some entertainment from the bartender, or do they just want to be left alone? Are they closing a business deal? Are they conducting a job interview? Is it a sales pitch, and, if so, can you help him out by making him look like a big shot?

Here's the rule: Read the customer and then err on the side of discretion. A customer who comes in for the third night in a row with a different date probably doesn't want you to mention that fact. A customer who rushes in every day around noon and throws down three quick martinis may not want to be recognized by you at all when the big boss takes her to your establishment for lunch.

On the other hand, many customers come to a bar specifically to engage in conversation with the bartender, and it is your job to satisfy them, whether they want sage advice, clever repartee, or outright abuse. Know who they are, know what they want, and let them have it. If you don't give them what they want, they'll go to another bartender who will.

Knowing the Customer

Closely related to reading the customer is knowing the customer. If a customer always asks you to make a Stoli martini straight up, in and out, twist of lemon, throw the twist out, save the rocks on the side, soda back with no ice and a lemon and a lime, she doesn't want to have to repeat this litany every single Friday at five-fifteen when she comes in. She wants to order "the usual," and she doesn't want the bartender to give her a blank look and say, "Huh?"

Suppose a customer always orders a bowl of soup at the bar. He asks you to heat it up in the microwave until it's scalding, then he lets it cool down to its original temperature so he can eat it without taking the skin off his tongue. Don't worry about it or comment on it.

Know your customers and give them what they want. Simple, isn't it? Nevertheless, many bartenders don't grasp the concept.

PRESSING THE FLESH

One evening I stopped in at a Chinese restaurant I'd never been in before. It was very nicely decorated, the lounge area in particular, with a half-moon-shaped bar made of dark marble and brass. Behind the bar was an older Chinese man named John, who wore his hair in a thick black pompadour like Elvis Presley.

While my take-out order was being prepared, I sat at the bar and ordered a Heineken, which the bartender poured into a frosty pilsner glass. Several other customers wandered in while I was waiting, and John called most of them by name as he reached over the bar and shook hands with them.

In no time at all the place was filled with a good-looking, well-heeled crowd, many of whom were dining at the bar. I got the distinct feeling that John was making quite a good living and had been for a while. The food was very good, and John's service was excellent, so about a month later I decided to try the place again. As I walked into the bar— my second time ever—John smiled at me, reached over the bar, and shook my hand. "Nice to see you again," he said.

A warm feeling came over me. I felt right at home. I pulled out a bar stool and sat down.

"Can I get you a Heineken this evening?" John asked.

Now that's a professional. He got a great deal of business from me over the next five years—until I moved away from the area—and I immediately put his simple technique to work in my own place of employment. I began greeting my own customers, the good ones, the big tippers, with a handshake. It may sound crazy, but I'm absolutely convinced it had a positive effect on business. My theory is that when new customers see you shaking hands with the regulars, they think, Hey, we want that cool bartender to shake hands with us and call us by our first names, too. We'd better come more often! And we'd better leave bigger tips!

Pressing the flesh works. Now, what about getting an Elvis hairstyle?

FOCUSING YOUR ATTENTION OUTWARD

Customers sitting at a bar, especially customers who are alone, notice everything. You may think that the man sitting there staring into his beer isn't listening as you and your co-workers huddle together behind the bar and bitch about the inhumane practices of a particular manager, or the lousy schedules you got that week, but he is listening—and he feels left out. While you enjoy camaraderie and conversation—maybe the very things he came in hoping to find—he sits there all alone in the world. Have a heart, will you?

If you're whispering to each other, customers will probably think you're talking about them. Well, okay, maybe you *are*. Maybe you're rolling your eyes and making snide little comments to your co-workers about stupid customers, but you think nobody notices. Well, I've got news for you: they do notice. Customers pick up these things, and they'll soon pick up their money and go somewhere else.

Keep your attention focused outward. Make an effort to include people at the bar in any discussions that spring up. Pay special attention to new customers. Your goal is to turn them into regular customers. It makes a big difference in the overall friendly atmosphere of a drinking establishment if the bartenders are focused outward on the customers and not inward on themselves.

TWELVE

THE BASIC
DRINKS

In the next chapter you will find recipes for some of the more unusual cocktails, but in reality the vast majority of cocktails you mix will be basic drinks. These are the recipes you *must* know if you want to call yourself a professional bartender.

MARTINIS AND MANHATTANS

Martini and manhattan drinkers are a special breed. They are serious drinkers, for one thing. Martinis and manhattans are made up of about two and a half ounces of liquor with no mixer! Customers who order them have acquired a taste for them, usually over a long period of time, and they want their drink made in a very specific manner. For many, drinking a martini or manhattan is a ritual that must be performed exactly the same way every time.

MARTINI

2¼ oz. gin
1⅛ oz. dry vermouth

1. Fill martini glass with ice to chill
2. Fill mixing glass with ice
3. Add gin and vermouth
4. Stir with a bar spoon
5. Empty ice from martini glass
6. Strain mixture into chilled martini glass
7. Garnish with olive or lemon twist

This is the classic martini of which there are many variations:

Dry Martini
Less vermouth is added.

Extra-Dry Martini
Only a few drops of vermouth are added.

Very, Very Extra-Dry, or Bone-Dry Martini
The vermouth bottle is waved over the glass so that only the vermouth fumes get into the cocktail and the customer is drinking 2¼ ounces of chilled gin.

In-and-Out Martini
The vermouth is poured over the ice that chills the martini glass, swirled around, and then dumped out before the gin is added so the vermouth only coats the glass.

Dirty Martini
About ¼ ounce olive juice, which is amber in color, is added to the martini. Sometimes bitters is used instead.

Straight up Martini
This drink is served in a glass with no ice. It is stirred, not shaken. James Bond may drink his martinis "shaken, not stirred," but nobody else does. Never shake a martini. The customer will ask for an olive or a lemon twist, or both.

Martini on the Rocks
This drink is built right in the serving glass, which is usually a 5-ounce rocks glass.

Vodka Martini
Vodka, rum or tequila is used instead of gin. All the same categories apply—dry vodka martini, extra-dry vodka martini, and so on.

Brand-name Martini
Customers will sometimes call for a Stoli martini on the rocks or an extra-dry Beefeater martini straight up.

Gibson
This is a very close relative of the martini, the only difference being the garnish. A Gibson is garnished with small cocktail onions. (It received its name long ago in a club in New York when a man named Gibson took to putting onions in his martinis.) All of the same variations apply here. For example, if somebody orders an extra-dry Absolut Gibson on the rocks, make an Absolut martini and throw in a couple cocktail onions.

The basic manhattan is made in a similar fashion to the martini, except that sweet vermouth and whiskey are used instead of dry vermouth and gin. It is made in a martini glass.

MANHATTAN

2¼ oz. rye whiskey
¼ oz. sweet vermouth

1. Fill martini glass with ice to chill
2. Fill mixing glass with ice
3. Add whiskey and sweet vermouth
4. Stir with a bar spoon
5. Empty ice from martini glass
6. Strain mixture into chilled martini glass
7. Garnish with a cherry

Variations on the basic manhattan, include the *Rob Roy*, which is made with Scotch instead of rye whiskey. (Remember that Rob Roy was the Robin Hood of Scotland.) The *perfect manhattan* contains equal parts (⅛ oz. each) of sweet *and* dry vermouth and gets a lemon twist instead of a cherry. (Remember that it takes two hands to twist a lemon, and this drink takes two vermouths.) A *dry manhattan* is made with only dry vermouth and always gets a lemon twist instead of a cherry. A *bourbon manhattan* is made with bourbon instead of rye whiskey.

Manhattans are often ordered with brand names: *perfect Canadian Club manhattan*, a *dry Dewar's Rob Roy* or an *Old Grand-Dad manhattan*. A manhattan on the rocks is built right in the serving glass, which is usually a 5-ounce rocks glass.

Highballs

These cocktails are served in 8-ounce or 10-ounce high-ball glasses. To make a highball, first fill the glass with ice. Then pour the liquor over the ice and add the mixer. (Sometimes you will add the liquor and mixer at the same time.) The highball glass should always be filled to the top with ice; otherwise it will take too much mixer to fill the glass, and the cocktail will taste weak. Highballs are never shaken or stirred by the bartender, although they are meant to be stirred by the customer.

THE HIGHBALL

1½ oz. rye whiskey
ginger ale

1. Fill highball glass with ice
2. Add rye whiskey
3. Fill with ginger ale
4. Serve with sip stick

GIN, VODKA, OR RUM AND TONIC

1½ oz. gin (vodka, rum)
tonic water

1. Fill highball glass with ice
2. Add gin (vodka, rum)
3. Fill with tonic water
4. Garnish with lime
5. Serve with sip stick

NOTE: Any cocktail made with tonic water automatically gets a lime wedge garnish

7&7

1½ oz. Seagram's 7
7Up

1. Fill highball glass with ice
2. Add Seagram's 7
3. Fill with 7Up
4. Serve with sip stick

SCOTCH (VODKA, BOURBON, WHISKEY) AND WATER

1½ Scotch (vodka, bourbon, whiskey)
water

1. Fill highball glass with ice
2. Add Scotch vodka, bourbon, whiskey
3. Fill with water
4. Serve with sip stick

NOTE: A drink ordered with "a splash" gets only a small amount of water and may be made in a smaller glass.

Notice that a highball is a specific cocktail and also a *type* of cocktail. Many other cocktails—whiskey and Coke, rum and Coke, Scotch and soda, Bourbon and ginger—are also highballs and are made the same way as the cocktails above.

Highballs are often called for by brand names: JD (Jack Daniel's) and Coke, Dewar's and soda, Bombay and Seven, T&T (Tanqueray and tonic), Black Label (Johnnie Walker Black) and water.

Basic Juice Drinks

Juice-based cocktails are made much the same way as high-balls. When there are combinations of juices in the recipe, a 50-50 mixture is used. All are made in highball glasses.

SCREWDRIVER

1½ oz. vodka
orange juice

1. Fill highball glass with ice
2. Add vodka
3. Fill with orange juice
4. Serve with a sip stick

GREYHOUND

1½ oz. vodka
grapefruit juice

1. Fill highball glass with ice
2. Add vodka
3. Fill with grapefruit juice
4. Serve with a sip stick

NOTE A Greyhound served in a glass with a salted rim is called a *Salty Dog*.

CAPE CODDER

1½ oz. vodka
cranberry juice

1. Fill highball glass with ice
2. Add vodka
3. Fill with cranberry juice
4. Garnish with a lime wedge
5. Serve with a sip stick

MEMORY AID: Cape Cod is famous for its cranberry bogs

MADRAS

1½ oz. vodka
orange juice
cranberry juice

1. Fill highball glass with ice
2. Add vodka
3. Fill with equal parts orange and cranberry juice
4. Serve with a sip stick

SEA BREEZE

1½ oz. vodka
grapefruit juice
cranberry juice

1. Fill highball glass with ice
2. Add vodka
3. Fill with equal parts cranberry and grapefruit juice
4. Garnish with lime wedge
5. Serve with a sip stick

HAWAIIAN SEA BREEZE (BAY BREEZE)

1½ oz. vodka
cranberry juice
pineapple juice

1. Fill highball glass with ice
2. Add vodka
3. Fill with equal parts cranberry and pineapple juice
4. Serve with sip stick

TEQUILA SUNRISE

1½ oz. tequila
½ oz. grenadine
orange juice

1. Fill a highball glass with ice
2. Add tequila
3. Fill with orange juice
4. Top with grenadine
5. Garnish with a cherry
6. Serve with a sip stick

The basic juice drinks are often ordered by brand name: Stoli screwdriver, Absolut madras, Smirnoff sea breeze. A Stoli with a splash of orange juice is served over ice in a 5-ounce rocks glass and is technically not a screwdriver. Always make sure the juices you are using are fresh.

Basic Cream Drinks

Cream cocktails are usually made in highball glasses when served over ice. Milk can be substituted for cream, and when cream is used it is usually light cream or half and half.

Milk or cream will separate from liquor, so the basic cream drinks are always shaken before they are served. Exceptions to this rule are the novelty cream drinks where layering of ingredients is desired.

When shaking a cream drink in the serving glass, place the small metal shaker cup over the glass. Shake the combination and place it back on the rail with the metal cup on the bottom. Remove the serving glass from the top and pour *from* the metal cup *into* the glass.

Some bartenders will place the combination back on the rail with the serving glass on the bottom and then remove the metal shaker cup off the top. This is not a good practice, especially with cream drinks, because the creamy mixture will run in a thin layer down the outside of the serving glass, making it very slippery. Pouring from metal into glass may be a split second slower, but the presentation is better and you won't look like a fool when the cocktail slips out of your hand and spills on the bar. Ever try to clean up spilled cream? Just remember, from metal to glass, never glass to glass. Make it a habit. It's a small detail, but many small details added together differentiate the pros from the amateurs.

SOMBRERO

1½ oz. Kahlúa
light cream

1. Fill highball glass with ice
2. Add Kahlúa

3. Fill with light cream
4. Shake
5. Serve with a sip stick

NOTE: A sombrero is a Mexican hat, and Kahlúa is made in Mexico.

WHITE RUSSIAN

1¼ oz. vodka into glass
¾ oz. Kahlúa
light cream

1. Fill highball glass with ice
2. Add vodka and Kahlúa
3. Fill with light cream
4. Shake
5. Serve with sip stick

MEMORY AID: Vodka originated in Russia

TOASTED ALMOND

¾ oz. Kahlúa
¾ oz. amaretto
light cream

1. Fill highball glass with ice
2. Add Kahlúa and amaretto
3. Fill with light cream
4. Shake
5. Serve with a sip stick

ROASTED TOASTED ALMOND

¾ oz. Kahlúa
¾ oz. amaretto
¾ oz. vodka
light cream

1. Fill highball glass with ice
2. Add Kahlúa, amaretto and vodka
3. Fill with light cream
4. Shake
5. Serve with sip stick

BRANDY ALEXANDER

1¼ oz. brandy
½ oz. dark crème de cacao
1½ oz. light cream

1. Fill martini glass with ice to chill
2. Fill mixing glass with ice
3. Add all ingredients to mixing glass
4. Shake
5. Empty ice from martini glass
6. Strain mixture into chilled martini glass
7. Sprinkle with nutmeg

Cream drinks can be called for by brand names: Stoli White Russian or Smirnoff White Russian. A sombrero is almost always called for as a Kahlúa sombrero.

Don't shake these cocktails too hard. The idea is to mix the cream and liquor, not put a frothy head on it like a Tom Collins. Check the cream frequently for freshness, as it can spoil quickly—Kahlúa does not mix well with cottage cheese.

BASIC FROZEN DRINKS

Frozen cocktails have become very popular in recent years. Originally associated with tropical resorts, they have become standard in all climates. At one time seasonal, they are now called for year-round. Once considered ladies' drinks, they are now ordered by everybody. Designed as afternoon-by-the-pool drinks, or dessert cocktails, they are now consumed before dinner or even with a meal. Some say this trend in the consumption of frozen drinks can be directly linked to the decline of American society.

If you work as a bartender in an establishment that features frozen cocktails, my advice is to get used to it. Don't cringe every time some big macho construction worker steps up to the bar and orders a frozen strawberry daiquiri. Act like a professional. Making these drinks is part of your job. You don't like it? Work somewhere else.

So what if they're a little more time-consuming to make? Develop repetitious moves, keep the blender tops rinsed out and near the blenders, have plenty of backup mix ready to go, and the task won't be so painful.

FROZEN DAIQUIRI

1½ oz. light rum
½ oz. Rose's lime juice
4 oz. sour mix

1. Place 1½ scoops of ice into blender
2. Add all ingredients
3. Blend all ingredients on high for thirty seconds
4. Pour mixture into large tulip glass
5. Garnish with lime wheel
6. Serve with a large drinking straw

FROZEN PIÑA COLADA

1½ oz. light rum
4 oz. piña colada mix

1. Place 1½ scoop of ice into blender
2. Add light rum and piña colada mix
3. Blend all ingredients on high for thirty seconds
4. Pour mixture into large tulip glass
5. Garnish with a slice of pineapple
6. Serve with a large drinking straw

FROZEN STRAWBERRY DAIQUIRI

1 oz. light rum
¾ oz. strawberry liqueur
4 oz. pureed strawberries

1. Place 1½ scoop ice into blender
2. Add light rum, strawberry liqueur and pureed
   strawberries
3. Blend all ingredients on high for thirty seconds
4. Pour mixture into large tulip glass
5. Garnish with a strawberry or orange flag
6. Serve with a large drinking straw

FROZEN MIDORI COLADA
(HONEYDEW MELON COLADA)

1½ oz. Midori
4 oz. piña colada mix

1. Place 1½ scoops ice into blender
2. Add Midori and piña colada mix
3. Blend all ingredients on high for thirty seconds
4. Pour mixture into large tulip glass
5. Garnish with orange flag
6. Serve with a large drinking straw

FROZEN MARGARITA

1½ oz. tequila
¾ oz. Triple Sec
¾ Rose's lime juice
3 oz. sour mix

1. Place 1½ scoops of ice into blender
2. Add all ingredients
3. Blend all ingredients on high for thirty seconds
4. Salt the rim of a large tulip glass
5. Pour mixture into salted tulip glass
6. Garnish with a lime wheel
7. Serve with a large drinking straw

FROZEN MUDSLIDE

1 oz. vodka
¾ oz. Kahlúa
¾ oz. Baileys Irish Cream
2 oz. light cream
vanilla ice cream

1. Place 1½ scoops of ice into a blender
2. Add one scoop of vanilla ice cream
3. Add vodka, Baileys Irish Cream and Kahlúa
4. Add light cream
5. Blend all ingredients on high for thirty seconds
6. Pour mixture into large tulip glass
7. Serve with a large drinking straw

FROZEN BANANA DAIQUIRI

1½ light rum
¾ banana liqueur
3 oz. light cream
fresh banana

1. Place 1½ scoops ice into blender
2. Add one half of a fresh banana
3. Add light cream
4. Blend all ingredients on high for thirty seconds
5. Pour mixture into a large tulip glass
6. Garnish with a cherry
7. Serve with a large drinking straw

There are many variations of these frozen drinks. The *frozen strawberry colada*, for instance, has half piña colada mix and half strawberry mix. The *frozen strawberry margarita* contains strawberry mix in place of lemon mix (sour mix), and the frozen Midori margarita contains Midori liqueur instead of Triple Sec. A *Chi Chi* is a frozen piña colada made with vodka instead of rum.

Nonalcoholic versions of many of these drinks are called virgins: the virgin strawberry daiquiri, virgin piña colada, and so on. They are made the same way, but without the alcohol. You may have to add a little water to make them blend smoothly—a little cranberry juice works well with the virgin strawberry daiquiri—or use crushed ice if it's available. Obviously, you can't make a virgin honeydew melon colada, because it is the alcohol that provides the honeydew flavor. Every now and then somebody will call for a virgin frozen margarita. Try to discourage this. The mixture of straight sour mix and Rose's lime juice blended with ice tastes terrible.

Serve the frozen margaritas as soon as possible after pouring into the glass. If they sit for a while they tend to separate, and the presentation will suffer.

When making frozen drinks as part of a large drink order, it is more efficient to get the frozen drink going in the blender first and use that time to make the other cocktails.

Make sure you rinse the blender cup well after using. If you follow up a frozen strawberry daiquiri with a frozen margarita without rinsing well, the margarita will be pink and you'll have to make it again. That hurts!

One last tip: If the frozen drink you are making won't pour out of the blender, run hot water over the outside of the blender or shoot a little cold water right *into* the blender and blend the drink again for a few seconds.

THE BLOODY MARY

Named after a queen of England, the Bloody Mary has become one of the most popular drinks served in bars today. This cocktail, which is often served as a brunch drink on Sunday mornings, is believed by some to be a remedy for a hangover.

BLOODY MARY

1½ oz. vodka
dash of pepper
dash of salt
2 dashes of Worcestershire sauce
dash of Tabasco sauce
¼ bar spoon horseradish
dash of celery salt
tomato juice

1. Fill large tulip glass with ice
2. Add vodka
3. Add spices
4. Fill with tomato juice
5. Shake gently
6. Garnish with celery stalk and lime wedge
7. Serve with large drinking straw

The Bloody Mary should be shaken gently or, better yet, poured from the serving glass into the metal shaker cup and then back into the serving glass. Do not shake it vigorously. If you are using a Bloody Mary base mix, simply add one spoonful along with the vodka, ice and tomato juice and then shake.

Fill the glass only two-thirds full of ice for this cocktail. You don't want the mix, which is very flavorful, to become diluted by melting ice.

Substitute clamato juice and you have a *Bloody Caesar*. Substitute tequila for vodka and you have a *Bloody Maria*. Throw in some beef bouillion and you have a *Bloody Bull*.

THIRTEEN

WHAT SHOULD I ORDER?

As a professional bartender you will often be confronted with the customer who sits down at the bar, rests her chin in her hand, and says, "Hmmm. I'm not sure what I want." She will look down at the floor and then up at the ceiling while you wait patiently. She will tap her fingers on the bar and scan the bottles on the shelves behind you. "I just don't know what I want," she will say. "I want something different. I want something . . ."

"I Want Something Fruity"

ALABAMA SLAMMER

1½ oz. Southern Comfort
1 oz. vodka
½ oz. sloe gin
½ oz. Triple Sec
orange juice

1. Fill a collins glass with ice
2. Add Southern Comfort, vodka, sloe gin and Triple Sec
3. Fill with orange juice
4. Shake
5. Garnish with a cherry
6. Serve with a large drinking straw

MEMORY AID: Alabama is in the south and the Crimson Tide is red, like sloe gin.

APRICOT SOUR

1½ oz. apricot brandy
sour mix

1. Fill a highball glass with ice
2. Add apricot brandy
3. Fill with sour mix
4. Shake
5. Garnish with an orange and cherry
6. Serve with a sip stick

BAHAMA MAMA

¾ oz. Malibu rum
¾ oz. dark rum
pineapple juice
cranberry juice

1. Fill highball glass with ice
2. Add Malibu rum and dark rum
3. Fill with equal parts pineapple juice and cranberry juice
4. Garnish with a lime wedge
5. Serve with a sip stick

BLUE HAWAIIAN

1½ oz. light rum
½ oz. blue curaçao
pineapple juice

1. Fill highball glass with ice
2. Add light rum and blue curaçao
3. Fill with pineapple juice
4. Garnish with a pineapple slice
5. Serve with a sip stick

BOCCI BALL

1½ oz. amaretto
orange juice

1. Fill highball glass with ice
2. Add amaretto
3. Fill with orange juice
4. Garnish with orange slice
5. Serve with a sip stick

MEMORY AID: Bocci is a game which originated in Italy, just like amaretto.

FREDDY FUDPUCKER

1½ oz. tequila
½ oz. Galliano
orange juice

1. Fill highball glass with ice
2. Add tequila
3. Fill with orange juice
4. Top with Galliano
5. Serve with a sip stick

MEMORY AID: Freddy Fudpucker is a close friend of Harvey Wallbanger

FUZZY NAVEL

1½ oz. peach schnapps
orange juice

1. Fill a highball glass with ice
2. Add peach schnapps
3. Fill with orange juice
4. Serve with a sip stick

MEMORY AID: A peach is fuzzy and an orange has a navel

GOLDEN PEACH

1½ oz. peach brandy
¾ oz. gin
orange juice

1. Fill a highball glass with ice
2. Add peach brandy and gin
3. Fill with orange juice
4. Serve with a sip stick

GRAPE CRUSH

¾ oz. Chambord
¾ oz. vodka
sour mix

1. Fill a highball glass with ice
2. Add Chambord and vodka
3. Fill with sour mix
4. Shake
5. Serve with a sip stick

HARVEY WALLBANGER

1½ oz. vodka
½ oz. Galliano
orange juice

1. Fill a highball glass with ice
2. Add vodka
3. Fill with orange juice
4. Top with Galliano
5. Serve with a sip stick

MEMORY AID: Galliano, because of the size of the bottle, is usually stored against the wall.

HAWAIIAN PUNCH

1½ oz. vodka
¼ oz. sloe gin
¼ oz. Southern Comfort
pineapple juice
orange juice

1. Fill a collins glass with ice
2. Add vodka, sloe gin and Southern Comfort
3. Fill with equal parts pineapple juice and orange juice
4. Shake
5. Serve with a large drinking straw

HOLLYWOOD

¾ oz. vodka
¾ oz. Chambord
pineapple juice

1. Fill a highball glass with ice
2. Add vodka and Chambord
3. Fill with pineapple juice
4. Serve with a sip stick

HOP, SKIP AND GO NAKED

1 oz. vodka
1 oz. rum
½ oz. Triple Sec
orange juice
pineapple juice

1. Fill a collins glass with ice
2. Add vodka, rum and Triple Sec
3. Fill with equal parts orange juice and pineapple juice
4. Garnish with orange flag
5. Serve with a large drinking straw

KILLER KOOL-AID

¾ oz. vodka
¾ oz. Midori
¾ oz. amaretto
cranberry juice

1. Fill a highball glass with ice
2. Add vodka, Midori and amaretto
3. Fill with cranberry juice
4. Serve with a sip stick

MAI TAI

1 oz. dark rum
1 oz. light rum
½ oz. Triple Sec
½ oz. apricot brandy
½ oz. Rose's lime juice
¼ oz. grenadine
pineapple juice
orange juice

1. Fill a large tulip glass with ice
2. Add rum, Triple Sec, apricot brandy and Rose's lime juice
3. Fill with orange and pineapple juice
4. Top with grenadine
5. Garnish with an orange flag
6. Serve with a large drinking straw

ORANGE CRUSH

1½ oz. Absolut citron
¾ oz. Galliano
¾ oz. Triple Sec
orange juice
7Up

1. Fill a highball glass with ice
2. Add Absolut citron, Galliano and Triple Sec
3. Fill with orange juice
4. Top with 7Up

PARK AVENUE

2 oz. gin
1 oz. sweet vermouth
1 oz. pineapple juice

1. Fill a mixing glass with ice
2. Add all ingredients
3. Shake
4. Strain into a cocktail glass

PEARL HARBOR

1½ oz. vodka
1 oz. Midori
pineapple juice

1. Fill a collins glass with ice
2. Add vodka and Midori
3. Fill with pineapple juice
4. Shake
5. Garnish with an orange slice
6. Serve with a large drinking straw

MEMORY AID: Midori comes from Japan, and pineapples come from Hawaii. Japan and Hawaii, get it?

PINEAPPLE BOMB

¾ oz. Southern Comfort
¾ oz. amaretto
pineapple juice

1. Fill a highball glass with ice
2. Add Southern Comfort and amaretto
3. Fill with pineapple juice
4. Serve with a sip stick

PLANTER'S PUNCH

1½ oz. dark rum
1 oz. light rum
dash bitters
orange juice
pineapple juice
sour mix
soda water

1. Fill a large tulip glass with ice
2. Add dark and light rum
3. Add bitters
4. Fill with equal parts orange juice, pineapple juice and
   sour mix
5. Shake
6. Top with soda water
7 Garnish with orange flag
8. Serve with a large drinking straw

SAN JUAN COOLER

2 oz. Bacardi Light
¾ oz. dry vermouth
pineapple juice

1. Fill a highball glass with ice
2. Add Bacardi Light and dry vermouth
3. Fill with pineapple juice
4. Serve with a sip stick

MEMORY AID: Bacardi comes from Puerto Rico, of which
San Juan is the capital.

SCARLET O'HARA

1½ oz. Southern Comfort
cranberry juice

1. Fill a highball glass with ice
2. Add Southern Comfort
3. Fill with cranberry juice
4. Serve with a sip stick

MEMORY AID: Scarlett O'Hara came from the South, like Southern Comfort, and cranberry juice is scarlet in color.

SEX ON THE BEACH

1 oz. vodka
¾ oz. peach schnapps
cranberry juice
orange juice

1. Fill a highball glass with ice
2. Add vodka and peach schnapps
3. Fill with equal parts cranberrry juice and orange juice
4. Serve with a sip stick

SLOE COMFORTABLE SCREW
AGAINST THE WALL

1 oz. sloe gin
1 oz. Southern Comfort
½ oz. Galliano
orange juice

1. Fill a highball glass with ice
2. Add sloe gin and Southern Comfort
3. Fill with orange juice
4. Top with Galliano
5. Serve with a sip stick

MEMORY AID: Sloe is sloe gin, Comfortable is Southern Comfort, Screw is orange juice, as in screwdriver, and Against the Wall refers to Galliano, which is usually stored against a wall because of the size of the bottle.

TEQUILA MOCKINGBIRD

1½ oz. tequila
½ oz. Triple Sec
orange juice
cranberry juice

1. Fill highball glass with ice
2. Add tequila and Triple Sec
3. Fill with equal parts orange juice and cranberry juice
4. Garnish with lime wedge
5. Serve with a sip stick

MEMORY AID: Triple Sec rhymes with Gregory Peck, who played Atticus in the movie version of Harper Lee's classic novel.

UNIVERSAL

1½ oz. vodka
1 oz. Midori
orange juice

1. Fill a highball glass with ice
2. Add vodka and Midori
3. Fill with orange juice
4. Shake
5. Garnish with an orange slice
6. Serve with a sip stick

WATERMELON

¾ oz. Midori
¾ oz. vodka
cranberry juice

1. Fill a highball glass with ice
2. Add Midori and vodka
3. Fill with cranberry juice
4. Serve with a sip stick

ZOMBIE

1½ oz. Bacardi 151
1 oz. dark rum
½ oz. amaretto
½ oz. Triple Sec
sour mix
orange juice
pineapple juice

1. Fill a large tulip glass with ice
2. Add Bacardi 151, amaretto, and Triple Sec
3. Fill with equal parts sour mix, pineapple juice, and
   orange juice
4. Shake
5. Top with dark rum
6. Garnish with orange flag
7. Serve with large drinking straw

"I Want Something Creamy"

AMARETTO CREAM

1½ oz. amaretto
cream

1. Fill rocks glass with ice
2. Add amaretto
3. Fill with cream
4. Shake
5. Serve with sip stick

BANANA BANSHEE

¾ oz. crème de bananes
¾ oz. white crème de cacao
cream

1. Fill highball glass with ice
2. Add crème de bananes and white crème de cacao
3. Fill with cream
4. Shake
5. Serve with sip stick

BARBARY COAST

¾ oz. gin
¾ oz. Scotch
¾ oz. dark crème de cacao
¾ oz. cream

1. Fill mixing glass with ice
2. Add all ingredients
3. Shake
4. Strain mixture into cocktail glass

BELMONT COCKTAIL

2 oz. gin
⅛ oz. grenadine
1 oz. cream

1. Fill mixing glass with ice
2. Add all ingredients
3. Shake
4. Strain mixture into cocktail glass

BRANDY PUFF

1½ oz. brandy
milk
soda water

1. Fill a highball glass with ice
2. Add brandy
3. Fill with milk
4. Shake
5. Top with soda water
6. Serve with a sip stick

BUBBLE GUM

1¼ oz. Southern Comfort
½ oz. crème de bananes
⅛ oz. grenadine
cream

1. Fill a highball glass with ice
2. Add Southern Comfort, crème de bananes and
   grenadine
3. Fill with cream
4. Shake
5. Serve with a sip stick

CARA SPOSA

1 oz. tequila
1 oz. Triple Sec
cream

1. Fill a rocks glass with ice
2. Add tequila and Triple Sec
3. Fill with cream
4. Shake
5. Serve with a sip stick

CHOCOLATE RUM

1 oz. light rum
½ oz. white crème de cacao
cream

1. Fill a rocks glass with ice
2. Add light rum and white crème de cacao
3. Fill with cream
4. Shake
5. Serve with a sip stick

COWBOY

3 oz. rye whiskey
½ oz. cream

1. Fill a mixing glass with ice
2. Add whiskey and cream
3. Shake
4. Strain mixture into cocktail glass

DIRTY FRIAR

1½ oz. Frangelico
¾ oz. vodka
cream

1. Fill a highball glass with ice
2. Add Frangelico and vodka
3. Fill with cream
4. Shake
5. Serve with a sip stick

MEMORY AID: Frangelico was supposedly invented by monks, or friars, and comes in a bottle shaped like a monk.

DIRTY WHITE MOTHER

1½ oz. brandy
¾ oz. Kahlúa
cream

1. Fill a rocks glass with ice
2. Add brandy and Kahlúa
3. Fill with cream
4. Shake
5. Serve with a sip stick

F&B

1 oz. Frangelico
1 oz. Baileys Irish Cream

1. Fill a rocks glass with ice
2. Add ingredients
3. Serve with a sip stick

FUDGSICKLE

1 oz. vodka
1 oz. dark crème de cacao
cream

1. Fill a rocks glass with ice
2. Add vodka and dark crème de cacao
3. Fill with cream
4. Serve with a sip stick

GIRL SCOUT COOKIE

1½ oz. Kahlúa
1 oz. peppermint schnapps
cream

1. Fill a highball glass with ice
2. Add Kahlúa and peppermint schnapps
3. Fill with cream
4. Shake
5. Serve with a sip stick

GOD CHILD

1½ oz. vodka
½ oz. amaretto
cream

1. Fill a rocks glass with ice
2. Add vodka and amaretto
3. Fill with cream
4. Shake
5. Serve with a sip stick

GOLDEN DREAM

1½ oz. Galliano
¾ oz. Triple Sec
½ oz. orange juice
½ oz. cream

1. Fill a mixing glass with ice
2. Add all ingredients
3. Shake
4. Strain mixture into a cocktail glass

GRASSHOPPER

1 oz. green crème de menthe
1 oz. white crème de cacao
1 oz. cream

1. Fill a mixing glass with ice
2. Add all ingredients
3. Shake
4. Strain mixture into a cocktail glass

MUDSLIDE

1 oz. vodka
¾ oz. Kahlúa
¾ oz. Baileys Irish Cream

1. Fill a rocks glass with ice
2. Add all ingredients
3. Serve with a sip stick

NUTCRACKER

1 oz. Kahlúa
1 oz. Baileys Irish Cream
1 oz. Frangelico

1. Fill a mixing glass with ice
2. Add all ingredients
3. Serve with a sip stick

NUTS AND BERRIES

¾ oz. Frangelico
¾ oz. Chambord
cream

1. Fill a mixing glass with ice
2. Add Frangelico and Chambord
3. Fill with cream
4. Shake
5. Serve with a sip stick

MEMORY AID: Frangelico is hazelnut-flavored and Chambord is raspberry-flavored

ORGASM

½ oz. vodka
½ oz. Triple Sec
½ oz. white crème de cacao
½ oz. amaretto
cream

1. Fill a highball glass with ice
2. Add vodka, Triple Sec, white crème de cacao and amaretto
3. Fill with cream
4. Shake
5. Garnish with two cherries on either side of a large straw

PANAMA COCKTAIL

1 oz. light rum
1 oz. white crème de cacao
1 oz. cream

1. Fill a mixing glass with ice
2. Add all ingredients
3. Shake
4. Strain mixture into a cocktail glass

PINK CREOLE

1½ oz. light rum
⅛ oz. Rose's lime juice
⅛ oz. grenadine
½ oz. cream

1. Fill a mixing glass with ice
2. Add all ingredients
3. Shake
4. Strain mixture into a cocktail glass
5. Garnish with a cherry

PINK SQUIRREL

1 oz. crème de noyau
1 oz. white crème de cacao
1 oz. cream

1. Fill a mixing glass with ice
2. Add all ingredients
3. Shake
4. Strain mixture into a cocktail glass

MEMORY AID: Crème de noyau is pink and nut-flavored and squirrels like nuts.

PINK LADY

2 oz. gin
⅛ oz. grenadine
½ oz. cream

1. Fill a mixing glass with ice
2. Add all ingredients
3. Shake
4. Strain mixture into a cocktail glass

PLATINUM BLONDE

1 oz. light rum
1 oz. Cointreau
½ oz. cream

1. Fill a mixing glass with ice
2. Add all ingredients
3. Shake
4. Strain mixture into a cocktail glass

RUSSIAN BEAR

1½ oz. vodka
1 oz. white crème de cacao
cream

1. Fill a rocks glass with ice
2. Add vodka and white crème de cacao
3. Fill with cream
4. Shake
5. Serve with a sip stick

RUSSIAN QUAALUDE

⅓ oz. Stolichnaya vodka
⅓ oz. Kahlúa
⅓ oz. Frangelico
⅓ oz. Baileys Irish Cream
cream

1. Fill a highball glass with ice
2. Add Stoli, Kahlúa, Frangelico and Baileys
3. Fill with cream
4. Shake
5. Serve with a sip stick

SMITH AND KEARNS

1 oz. vodka
1 oz. Kahlúa
cream
soda water

1. Fill a highball glass with ice
2. Add vodka and Kahlúa
3. Fill with cream
4. Shake
5. Top with soda water
6. Serve with a sip stick

SNOWBALL

1½ oz. gin
½ oz. anisette
cream

1. Fill a rocks glass with ice
2. Add gin and anisette
3. Fill with cream
4. Serve with a sip stick

TOOTSIE ROLL

1½ oz. Kahlúa
3 oz. orange juice
½ oz. cream

1. Fill a highball glass with ice
2. Add all ingredients
3. Shake
4. Serve with a sip stick

TOREADOR

1½ oz. tequila
½ oz. dark crème de cacao
½ oz. cream
whipped cream

1. Fill a mixing glass with ice
2. Add tequila, dark crème de cacao and cream
3. Shake
4. Strain mixture into a cocktail glass
5. Top with whipped cream

VELVET HAMMER

¾ oz. Triple Sec
¾ oz. white crème de cacao
2 oz. cream

1. Fill a mixing glass with ice
2. Add all ingredients
3. Shake
4. Strain mixture into a cocktail glass

WHITE BULL

¾ oz. tequila
¾ oz. Kahlúa
cream

1. Fill a rocks glass with ice
2. Add tequila and Kahlúa
3. Fill with cream
4. Shake
5. Serve with a sip stick

MEMORY AID: Tequila and Kahlúa both come from Mexico, where they do a lot of bull fighting.

WHITE MINK

1½ oz. Galliano
¼ oz. brandy
¼ oz. white crème de cacao
1 oz. cream

1. Fill a mixing glass with ice
2. Add all ingredients
3. Shake
4. Strain mixture into a cocktail glass

"I Want Something Hot"

AMARETTO CAFE

1½ oz. amaretto
hot black coffee
whipped cream

1. Pour amaretto into a coffee mug
2. Fill with hot black coffee
3. Top with whipped cream
4. Serve with a sip stick

BAILEYS AND COFFEE

1½ oz. Baileys Irish Cream
hot black coffee

1. Pour Baileys Irish Cream into a coffee mug
2. Fill with hot black coffee
3. Serve with a sip stick

COFFEE ALEXANDER

¾ oz. brandy
¾ oz. dark crème de cacao
hot black coffee
whipped cream

1. Pour brandy and dark crème de cacao into a coffee mug
2. Fill with hot black coffee
3. Top with whipped cream
4. Sprinkle with nutmeg
5. Serve with a sip stick

DUTCH COFFEE

1½ oz. Vandermint
hot black coffee
whipped cream

1. Pour Vandermint into a coffee mug
2. Fill with hot black coffee
3. Top with whipped cream
4. Serve with a sip stick

MEMORY AID: Vandermint is a Dutch liqueur.

FRENCH COFFEE

¾ oz. cognac
¾ oz. Cointreau
hot black coffee
whipped cream

1. Pour cognac and Cointreau into a coffee mug
2. Fill with hot black coffee
3. Top with whipped cream
4. Serve with a sip stick

MEMORY AID: Cognac and Cointreau are both products of France

HOT BUTTERED RUM

1½ oz. light rum
1 teaspoon sugar
1 pat (1 tablespoon) butter
1 cup of hot water
1 cinnamon stick

1. Pour rum into a large brandy snifter
2. Add sugar
3. Add hot water
4. Add butter and cinnamon stick

HOT TODDY

1½ oz. whiskey
1 teaspoon sugar
hot water
lemon wedge

1. Pour whiskey into a coffee mug
2. Add sugar
3. Fill with hot water
4. Squeeze one lemon wedge and drop it into the mug

IRISH COFFEE

1½ oz. Irish whiskey
1 teaspoon sugar
⅛ oz. green crème de menthe
hot black coffee
whipped cream

1. Pour whiskey into a coffee mug
2. Add sugar
3. Fill with hot black coffee
4. Top with whipped cream
5. Dribble green crème de menthe on top of whipped cream
6. Serve with a sip stick

ITALIAN COFFEE

1½ oz. Sambuca
hot black coffee
whipped cream

1. Pour Sambuca into a coffee mug
2. Fill with hot black coffee
3. Top with whipped cream
4. Serve with a sip stick

MEMORY AID: Sambuca is a product of Italy

JAMAICAN COFFEE

1 oz. Tia Maria
½ oz. Myers's rum
hot black coffee
whipped cream

1. Pour Tia Maria and Myers's into a coffee mug
2. Fill with hot black coffee
3. Top with whipped cream
4. Serve with a sip stick

MEMORY AID: Both Myers's and Tia Maria are products of
Jamaica, *mon.*

KEOKE COFFEE

¾ oz. brandy
¾ oz. Kahlúa
¾ oz. Cointreau
hot black coffee
whipped cream

1. Pour brandy, Kahlúa and Cointreau into a coffee mug
2. Fill with hot black coffee
3. Top with whipped cream
4. Serve with a sip stick

"I WANT SOME KIND OF A SHOT"

ANGEL TIP

1 oz. white crème de cacao
⅓ oz. cream

1. Pour white crème de cacao into a cordial glass
2. Float the cream on top of the white crème de cacao by pouring it slowly over the back of a bar spoon so the two liquids do not mix
3. Garnish with a cherry on a toothpick centered across the top

B-52

⅓ oz. Kahlúa
⅓ oz. Baileys Irish Cream
⅓ oz. Grand Marnier

1. Pour Kahlúa into a cordial glass
2. Float Baileys by pouring slowly over the back of a bar spoon so the two liqueurs do not mix
3. Float Grand Marnier in the same manner so you end up with three distinct layers

BEAM ME UP SCOTTY

¾ oz. banana liqueur
¾ oz. Baileys Irish Cream
¾ oz. Kahlúa

1. Pour all ingredients into a rocks glass with no ice

BRAIN

1½ oz. Baileys Irish Cream
¾ oz. strawberry schnapps

1. Pour Baileys into a rocks glass with no ice
2. Add strawberry schnapps

BUTTER BALL

⅔ oz. butterscotch schnapps
⅓ oz. Baileys Irish Cream

1. Pour butterscotch schnapps into a cordial glass
2. Float Baileys on top by pouring slowly over the back of a bar spoon so the two liquors do not mix

CEMENT MIXER

1 oz. Baileys Irish Cream
¾ oz. Rose's lime juice

1. Pour Baileys into a rocks glass with no ice
2. Add Rose's lime juice

NOTE: The person doing this shot allows the two ingredients to mix in her mouth. It will thicken.

FIREBALL

1 oz. cinnamon schnapps
½ oz. cherry brandy
1 dash Tabasco sauce

1. Pour all ingredients into a rocks glass with no ice

GREEN LIZARD

1 oz. Chartreuse
½ oz. Bacardi 151

1. Pour ingredients into a rocks glass with no ice

HARBOR LIGHT

½ oz. Kahlúa
⅓ oz. Southern Comfort
⅓ oz. Bacardi 151

1. Pour ingredients into a rocks glass with no ice

JELLY BEAN

½ oz. anisette
½ oz. blackberry brandy

1. Pour anisette into a cordial glass
2. Float blackberry brandy on top by pouring it slowly over the back of a bar spoon so the two liqueurs do not mix

KAMIKAZE

1½ oz. vodka
¾ oz. Triple Sec
½ oz. Rose's lime juice

1. Fill a mixing glass with ice
2. Add all ingredients
3. Shake
4. Strain mixture into a rocks glass
5. Garnish with a lime wedge

LEMON DROP

1½ oz. Absolut citron
¼ oz. Rose's lime juice

1. Place sugar around the rim of a rocks glass
2. Add ingredients

PRAIRIE FIRE

1½ oz. tequila
dash of Tabasco sauce

1. Pour tequila into a rocks glass with no ice
2. Add Tabasco

PURPLE HOOTER

½ oz. vodka
½ oz. Chambord
½ oz. Triple Sec
¼ oz. Rose's lime juice

1. Fill a mixing glass with ice
2. Add all ingredients
3. Shake
4. Strain mixture into a rocks glass with no ice

SNOW SHOE

1 oz. bourbon
½ oz. peppermint schnapps

1. Pour ingredients into a rocks glass with no ice

SLIPPERY NIPPLE

¾ oz. Sambuca
¼ oz. Baileys Irish Cream

1. Pour Sambuca into a cordial glass
2. Float Baileys by pouring it slowly over the back of a
   bar spoon so the two liqueurs do not mix

STARS AND STRIPES

⅓ oz. grenadine
⅓ oz. cream
⅓ oz. blue curaçao

1. Pour grenadine into a cordial glass
2. Float cream by pouring it slowly over the back of a
   bar spoon
3. Float blue curaçao on top by pouring it slowly over the
   back of a bar spoon so you end up with three layers

VULCAN MIND BENDER

¾ oz. ouzo
¼ oz. Bacardi 151

1. Pour ouzo into a cordial glass
2. Float Bacardi 151 by pouring it slowly over the back of a bar spoon so the two liquids do not mix

WINDEX

1½ oz. vodka
½ oz. blue curaçao

1. Fill a mixing glass with ice
2. Add ingredients
3. Shake
4. Strain mixture into a rocks glass with no ice

WOO WOO

¾ oz. vodka
¾ oz. peach schnapps
1 oz. cranberry juice

1. Fill a mixing glass with ice
2. Add all ingredients
3. Shake
4. Strain mixture into a rocks glass with no ice

FOURTEEN

Bartenders' Magic Tricks And Puzzles

Occasionally you will be called upon to entertain your customers, and during the slow periods you might want to amuse your fellow employees. Here are a few ways to get the job done.

The Disappearing Martini

Prepare for this trick ahead of time by stuffing a thick wad of napkins or a dry bar towel into the bottom of the metal shaker cup. This will absorb any liquid you pour into the cup. Leave the mixing cup in its normal position so you can casually pick it up when you start the trick and nobody will know that it's been tampered with.

When you're ready to work your magic, simply fill a martini glass with ice and water and set it on the rail to chill. Then fill the large metal mixing cup with a heaping scoop of ice and set it on the rail next to the glass. Using a jigger to measure, pour a shot of gin into the mixing cup. Add a few drops of dry vermouth, and announce that this is an extra, extra dry disappearing martini. Give it a brief stir with the bar spoon and set the strainer on top of it. Then, make a few passes over it with the bar spoon while speaking the magic words: "Absolut vodka and Tanqueray gin, Magic Spirit, I'm calling you in. For Stolichnaya and the queen of Bombay, come and take this martini away!"

At the word "away," whack the strainer with the bar spoon. Dump the ice out of the martini glass, which is nice and chilled now, and strain the liquor from the metal mixing cup into the glass . . . but nothing comes out! The martini has disappeared!

Make elaborate movements and talk continuously to divert attention as you perform this trick. Dump the ice and the bar towel out into sink immediately after you finish.

Practice it a couple times before showing it to anybody. The real fun will come when you refuse to show your customers how you did it!

The Olive and the Snifter

Place an olive on the bar next to a snifter. The object of this trick is to get the olive inside the snifter without touching the olive or blowing on it.

Here's how you proceed: Place the snifter upside down over the olive. Swirl the snifter around, keeping it in contact with the surface of the bar, and the olive will fly up inside. Turn the snifter over quickly and stop swirling.

This trick will work *only with a snifter* because of the unique balloon shape of the glass. If you try it with a wineglass you will sling the olive halfway across the room.

Practice it a couple times before you show it to anybody. You might not be able to do it on your very first try, but you'll get the hang of it.

Boxes

Set up twelve matchsticks or toothpicks like this:

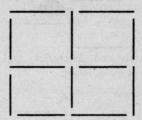

Notice there are five boxes here—four small ones and one large one. The object is to reposition three matchsticks so there are only three boxes. Here's the solution:

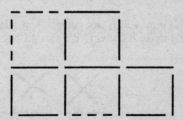

The Field Goal

Use matchsticks and an olive to demonstrate how your field goal kicker missed this field goal low and to the right.

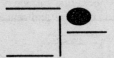

Can you move only two matchsticks and make the field goal good? Here is the solution:

Matchsticks for Mathematicians

Set up eighteen matchsticks like this:

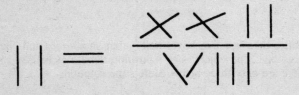

Obviously, this equation is not correct. Can you move *one* matchstick and make it correct? It's simple, once you know the solution:

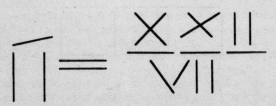

The Falling Matchbox

Here's a neat little challenge. Hold a standard box of matches three inches above the surface of the bar. Can you drop it so that it lands on edge and remains standing?

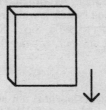

This trick is almost impossible to do unless you first open the end where the heads of the matches are, just a little bit, and it will act like a shock absorber. This might take some practice, but you'll get the hang of it.

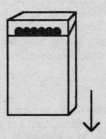

Heads I Win, Tails You Lose

A situation arises when you need to flip a coin to make a decision. Let's say it's a slow evening, so one of the bartenders will get to go home early, and you have to decide which one. Well, a matchbox will do just as well as a coin, won't it?

On one side of the matchbox is the logo of the establishment; that's heads. The other side shows the address and phone number; that's tails. You call heads. You flip the matchbook up in the air and let it land on the bar. Heads it is. Want to go two out of three? Heads again. See you later, pal. Have a nice night.

The trick is to slide a quarter underneath the little drawer in the matchbox, opposite the side that's heads, and it'll come up heads nine times out of ten. Put it in your pocket right after the flip and switch it with an unweighted box if your co-worker wants to see it. Say, "So long, sucker," as you pass by the bar on your way out the front door.

Gotcha

When a drinking establishment is not busy, maybe in mid-afternoon or during a blizzard, the waiters will congregate near the service bar, if for no other reason than to be close to the bartenders, whom they look up to and admire.

The night before, you will have placed a highball glass full of cranberry juice in the beer glass chiller so that it is now frozen solid. Place the highball glass on the service bar. When a waiter comes over, move your hand spastically and "accidentally" knock it over toward the waiter. Watch him jump! Watch him spring back into two other waiters and cause an interesting domino effect. Gotcha!

A Fine Vintage

When one of the waiters asks to sample the new wines that you are pouring by the glass, pull out the bottles and line up a few wineglasses. In a minute or two, like moths to a flame, half the wait staff will hurry over to the service bar to try the new wines, ostensibly so they can form an opinion and do a better job of selling wine to the customers at the tables, but in reality hoping to swallow half a glass in the process and maybe catch a little buzz.

While the swirling, sipping, smacking of lips and tossing around of adjectives is going on, select your victim. Pass him the special glass. Watch as he inspects the fine pale color. Watch as he quaffs it down. Watch as he gags and runs to the bathroom. That was a fine vintage, all right. Cocktail onion juice, right out of the bottle! Talk about a bold taste and a long finish!

A Disgusting Way To Get A Free Drink

You're sitting in the bar next door after a lousy night at work during which you made hardly any money. You want a nightcap, but you have no money left, so you turn to the customer next to you and make a little wager. Place four matchsticks in front of him on the bar and four in front of you. Tell him you'll buy him a shot of whiskey if he can duplicate everything you do with your matchsticks. If he can't duplicate what you do, he buys the shots. Your friend has confidence in himself. He agrees.

You order two shots of whiskey. The bartender brings them over, and you put one in front of you and one in front of your friend. You push one matchstick out on the bar in front of you next to the shot glass; he does the same. You push another matchstick out there at right angles to the first one; he does the same. You push another one out there, so now you have three sides of a square around the shot glass; he does the same. You push the fourth one out there, forming the fourth side of a little square with the shot glass in the middle; he does the same. You pick up the shot glass with your right hand, switch it to your left hand, switch it back to your right hand, drink the whiskey and very, very carefully replace it on the bar inside the little square; he does exactly the same. He grins at you. Now squirt the whiskey, *which you didn't swallow*, back into the shot glass. You win! Drink your shot (again), pat your new friend on the back, and go home.

Now You See 'Em, Now You Don't

Draw dots on two paper matchsticks with a pen, like this:

Now hold them in a parallel position between your thumb and forefinger. Turn your hand over to show the sides of the matches that don't have dots. Turn your hand over again to show the sides of the matches that have the dots. But wait! The dots are gone! Turn your hand over again. Look! The dots are on that side now! Turn your hand over again and they're gone. Now the dots are on both sides! Now you can't find them on either side!

The trick is to flip the matches between your thumb and forefinger *while* you turn your hand over. It takes a little practice to flip them simultaneously, but once you master the technique, your maneuver is impossible to detect. Keeps the kids amused.

FIFTEEN

BARTENDERS' JOKES

Every bartender needs a repertoire of jokes. That requirement comes with the territory. Here are a few good ones I've heard over the years, most of which can be told in mixed company. Tell them *before* the customer pays the tab. Adapt these jokes to your style, but please don't drag them out too long. Those customers at the other end of the bar need some attention, too.

The Mean Drunk

A well-dressed man comes into an establishment and sits down at the bar.

"Give me a shot of Jack Daniel's sour mash whiskey, if you would, sir," he says. "And while you're at it, pour a shot for each and every one of these fine people at the bar. Come to think of it, pour a shot for all those fine folks at the tables. And, Mr. Bartender, pour one for yourself, too."

So the bartender pours the shots, and when all of the

customers have theirs in front of them, the man raises his glass and says, "Here's to good health and a long, happy life!"

"Here, here!" the customers yell, and everybody, including the bartender, downs the whiskey.

The bartender says to the man, "Thank you, sir. That will be sixty-four dollars and fifty cents, please."

"I'm terribly sorry," the man says. "I don't have any money."

"What do you mean?" the bartender says, slightly perturbed. "I said that will be sixty-four dollars and fifty cents!"

"I'm terribly sorry," the man says again. "I don't have any money."

The bartender becomes angry. He comes out from behind the bar, grabs the man by the seat of the pants, and hurls him through the front door. The man goes sprawling across the sidewalk, slides face-first through a puddle, and ends up in a pile of rotten garbage.

The bartender goes back inside. About ten minutes later, much to his surprise, the man comes back in and sits down at the bar. His clothes are all wet and torn, and he reeks of garbage.

"Give me a shot of Jack Daniel's sour mash whiskey, if you would, sir," he says. "And while you're at it, pour a shot for each and every one of these fine people at the bar. Come to think of it, pour a shot for all those fine folks at the tables, too. But Mr. Bartender, none for you. You become quite violent when you drink."

Gorillas In the Irish Mist

One day when I was bartending, a gorilla came in and sat down at the bar. Didn't say a word, just pointed at the bottle of Irish Mist, so I poured a shot for him. Business was slow—matter of fact, he was the only customer at the bar—and he didn't appear too intelligent, so I charged him double. He finished his first drink and pointed at his glass, so I poured him another one, and I figured, what the hell, so

I charged him double again. Not a bad racket. Finally my curiosity started to get to me.

"Do you live in the neighborhood?" I said. "We don't generally get too many gorillas in here."

"That doesn't surprise me one little bit," the gorilla said. "The way the prices are in this joint!"

The Hustler

A man walked into a pub and sat on a stool at the bar. The bartender served him a beer, and a little while later the man called the bartender over and asked him if he would like to make a small wager.

"I'll bet you twenty-five dollars that I can lick my eye," the man said.

"That's a little steep for me," the bartender said. "That's almost half of what I make in a night. But then again, I don't think I've ever seen anybody do that." He stuck his tongue out, just to check how difficult it was. "Okay, I'll take the bet!"

The man promptly took out his glass eye, licked it and collected the money from the bartender. The bartender went back about his work in a dejected mood. A little while later the man waved him over again.

"Look," the man said. "You work hard for your money and I feel bad about taking it from you like that. Least I can do is give you a chance to win it back. Tell you what. You put a shot glass down on the other end of the bar, and I'll bet you twenty-five bucks that I can spit into that shot glass and not miss a drop."

The bartender, excited about the prospect of getting his money back, set the shot glass way down on the other end of the bar and stood back to watch. The man worked up a mouthful of saliva, turned, and spit right in the bartender's face. The bartender was so happy that he'd won his money back that he jumped up and down for joy while grinning from ear to ear. The man handed him his twenty-five dollars, walked down to another customer at the far end of the bar, collected five twenty-dollar bills from him, and kept on going right out the door.

"Hey, what was that all about?" the bartender asked the customer who had just shelled out the five twenties.

"That darned hustler!" the customer replied. "I met him on the way in here. He bet me a hundred bucks he could spit in your face and you'd be happy about it!"

The Critic

One afternoon a man came into a tavern and sat at the bar with his dog. The TV was on and tuned in to an old movie. The dog sat on a stool next to its master, and after a minute or two it was clear that the dog was watching the movie. He growled when the bad guy was on the screen; he whimpered and whined during the sad parts. When it came to the happy ending, the dog yelped joyously and wagged his tail.

"Gee whillickers," the bartender said. "It was really just amazing the way your dog reacted to that old movie. I've never seen anything quite like it."

"I have to tell you, I was pretty surprised myself," the customer said. "He hated the book!"

Bad Choice of Words

We happened to stop in at this one particular corner pub over on the West Side, one we'd never been in before. It was a busy place, and there were two bartenders behind the bar, two big burly fellows who bore a striking resemblance to each other, except that one of them had a very small head.

Now, I'm not talking about a below-average-size head. I'm talking about a very, *very* small head. So small that it looked absurd up there on those big, broad shoulders. The regulars at the bar were studiously pretending they hadn't noticed it, but my friend and I couldn't help staring.

Eventually the other bartender came over, leaned across the bar real close to us, and spoke in a low voice. "I know what you two are doing," he said. "You're staring at my brother Timmy's deformity. We'd appreciate it if you didn't gawk. He's not used to it yet, and he's still a bit sensitive about it."

"Gee," my friend said. "What happened?"

"I'll tell you," the bartender said, "if you promise not to stare."

So we promised, but it wasn't easy. We couldn't help wondering where he got that little tiny baseball cap.

"It happened last week," the bartender said. "Timmy was downstairs cleaning out the basement, and he comes across this old bottle. It's all dusty like, so he rubs it, figuring he'll look at the label, see what it is. Well, he rubs it, and then he pulls out the cork to see what it smells like, and out comes this genie."

"A genie?" we said.

"A genie," the bartender said. "A beautiful female genie, with long, flowing hair. She was wearing almost no clothes at all, and what she did have on, you could see right through. And she says to Timmy, 'You've freed me from the prison where I've been held captive for centuries. In order to show my gratitude I will grant you one wish.' So Timmy, being the way he is, never thinking too far ahead, he says, 'I'd like to make love with you, you beautiful genie.' So the genie says, 'Alas, that is the one wish I cannot grant. It is forbidden.' So Timmy says, 'Okay then, how about giving me a little head?' "

To Each His Own

Three male rabbits were being held captive in a scientific laboratory. Finally they couldn't stand it any longer and they decided to break out. Late one night they chewed through the locks on their cages, jumped out a window, and tunneled underneath a wall. Then they hopped and hopped all through the night and eventually collapsed from exhaustion and fell asleep.

When the morning came and they woke up, they discovered they were in a gigantic field of carrots. Carrots and nothing but carrots as far as the eye could see. So all day they ate carrots, as many as they could fit in their stomachs, and that night they fell asleep in the field, fat and happy.

The next morning they woke up and hopped over the next hill, and there below them in the valley was a herd of female rabbits. Nothing but female rabbits as far as the eye could see. So they hopped down there, and all morning they multiplied with the female rabbits, and all afternoon and into the evening until they collapsed from exhaustion and fell asleep, happy and satisfied.

The next morning when they woke up, the first rabbit turns to his friends and says, "You know, I'm going to stay right here in this valley with these female rabbits, and I'm going to multiply all day again. I think I missed a few yesterday."

The second rabbit says, "Not me. I had enough of that to hold me for a while. I'm going back to that field of carrots, and I'm going to eat until I can't eat anymore. That's what I think I'll do today."

The third rabbit turns to the first two and says, "Not me fellas, not me. I . . . I gotta get back to the lab."

"What!" they screamed. "Are you crazy? You're going to go back to the laboratory?"

"Sorry fellas, but I'm going crazy," the third rabbit says. "Jeez, I haven't had a cigarette in three days!"

Marital Bliss

The other day I was driving down Route 84 through Hartford with my wife, Frances, when we get pulled over by a state cop, lights flashing, siren going, the works. The cop walks up to my window and says, "Sir, do you know why I stopped you?"

I told him I had no idea.

"You were doing ninety miles an hour in a fifty-five-mile-an-hour zone," he says.

"Officer, no way," I say. "I was maybe doing sixty-five, tops, just keeping up with the traffic. Reason I know, the front end of this heap starts to vibrate when I get up around sixty-five, so I never go faster than that. Something must be wrong with your radar gun, or it's some kind of mistake.''

He seems to be buying it, but then Frances leans forward and says, ''Oh, no, Officer. He was going ninety, all right. I saw the speedometer. He was definitely going ninety, if not even faster.''

I couldn't believe it.

''Thank you, ma'am,'' the cop says, and he goes back to the cruiser to write up the ticket.

''You witch!'' I scream at Frances. ''What are you doing? Are you out of your mind? That's going to be three hundred bucks! Are you crazy?''

So the cop writes the ticket, and when he comes back to my window he says, ''And furthermore, sir, I'm going to have to cite you for not wearing your seat belt.''

''Wait a second,'' I said. ''Wait just a second. I *was* wearing my seat belt. I had it on, but then you pulled me over, and while you were walking up to the car I took it off because I knew I'd have to reach for my license and registration. See what I mean? I had it on, I swear. I always wear my seat belt. Wouldn't go down my driveway without my seat belt on.''

''Oh, no, Officer,'' Frances chimes in. ''He positively did not have his seat belt on. As a matter of fact, he thinks it's a stupid law, and he *never* wears his seat belt.''

''Thank you, ma'am,'' the cop says, and he proceeds to write me up another ticket right there.

''You . . . you *witch*!'' I scream. ''What in God's name are you doing? Are you out of your cotton-pickin' mind? Have you completely lost your marbles?''

The cop leans in my window. ''Excuse me, ma'am,'' he says. ''Does you husband always talk to you in this manner?''

Frances gets that little grin on her face. ''Oh, no, not all the time, Officer,'' she says in that sweet voice of hers. ''Only when he's been drinking.''

SIXTEEN

THE BARTENDERS' SUPER TRIVIA QUIZ

1. In what country is Drambuie made?
   a. U.S.A.
   b. Scotland
   c. Italy
   d. England

2. Which of the following cocktails is never served frozen?
   a. Mudslide
   b. Daiquiri
   c. Golden margarita
   d. Cuba libra

3. Which of the following liquors has the highest proof?
   a. Jim Beam
   b. Smirnoff vodka (red label)
   c. Johnnie Walker Black Label
   d. Rumple Mintz

4. Which of the following has alcohol in it?
   a. Rose's lime juice
   b. Sour mix
   c. Grenadine
   d. Angostura bitters

5. Which of the following is *not* a fruit-flavored liqueur?
   a. Midori
   b. Chambord
   c. Metaxa
   d. Triple Sec

6. What famous woman is pictured on the Bombay gin bottle?
   a. Queen Victoria
   b. Queen Elizabeth II
   c. Indira Gandhi
   d. Isabelle "Boodles" Tanqueray

7. Which country is the largest producer of beer in the world?
   a. Russia
   b. U.S.A.
   c. Japan
   d. Germany

8. Which of the following beverages is *not* traditionally consumed at room temperature?
   a. Burgundy
   b. Stout
   c. Lager
   d. Porter

9. Which of the following cocktails is never shaken?
   a. B-52
   b. Whiskey sour
   c. Sombrero
   d. Long Island iced tea

10. Which of the following is a liqueur?
    a. Southern Comfort
    b. Courvoisier
    c. Wild Turkey
    d. Absolut citron

11. Which of the following is *not* named after a country, province, or region?
    a. Anisette
    b. Tequila
    c. Bourbon
    d. Cognac

12. In what country is Midori made?
    a. Italy
    b. Spain
    c. Japan
    d. Mexico

13. Grenadine is used in all the following cocktails *except*:
    a. Shirley Temple
    b. Tequila Sunrise
    c. Bacardi Cocktail
    d. Scarlett O'Hara

14. When a customer orders a drink "neat," it means:
    a. It has no ice
    b. You stand up straight while you make it
    c. It contains only one liquor
    d. It is made in a tall glass

15. Benedictine was invented by:
    a. Nuns
    b. Monks
    c. Indians
    d. Capitalists

16. The first person to blend whiskey was:
    a. Jack Daniel
    b. Dean Martin
    c. William Dewar
    d. Andrew Usher

17. The best time to ask to see a manager of a drinking establishment about applying for a job is:
    a. 2:00 A.M.
    b. 3:00 P.M.
    c. 12:30 P.M.
    d. 5:30 P.M.

18. Molasses is used to produce which of the following?
    a. Rum
    b. Vodka
    c. Grenadine
    d. Bitters

19. A speed pourer is best described as:
    a. A fast bartender
    b. A beer tap
    c. A spout
    d. A jigger

20. What type of liquor is Justerini & Brooks most famous for?
    a. Scotch
    b. Gin
    c. Sambuca
    d. Rum

21. Which beverage comes in only one color?
    a. Crème de menthe
    b. Campari
    c. Rum
    d. Crème de cacao

22. Which glass has the largest capacity?
    a. Highball glass
    b. Rocks glass
    c. Martini glass
    d. Collins glass

23. When an obviously intoxicated customer orders a cocktail, the bartender should:
    a. Give him one more and hope he leaves
    b. Offer him a nonalcoholic beverage and ask to collect the tab
    c. Give him a watered-down cocktail and call the manager
    d. Ask him to leave and call the police

24. A liquor that is 86 proof is:
    a. 86 percent alcohol
    b. 68 percent alcohol
    c. 43 percent alcohol
    d. 14 percent alcohol

25. Which of the following is *not* orange flavored?
    a. Cointreau
    b. Grand Marnier
    c. Triple Sec
    d. Metaxa 7 Star

26. Which of the following is *not* bourbon?
    a. Jim Beam
    b. Jack Daniel's
    c. Wild Turkey
    d. Old Grand-Dad

27. Which of the following does *not* have a distinctive aroma?
    a. Stolichnaya vodka
    b. Bombay gin
    c. Rumple Mintz
    d. Grand Marnier

28. Which of the following is a blended Scotch?
    a. Canadian Club
    b. Glenlivet
    c. Johnnie Walker Black Label
    d. Old Bushmills

29. When a customer orders a perfect manhattan you:
    a. Do not stir it
    b. Use whiskey and dry vermouth
    c. Strain it through your fingers
    d. Use sweet and dry vermouth

30. What is the primary grain used in the making of Seagram's 7?
    a. Corn
    b. Barley
    c. Rye
    d. Wheat

31. Which of the following is *not* used to distill alcohol?
    a. Bananas
    b. Sugarcane
    c. Agave plants
    d. Rice

32. Sparkling wine sparkles because of:
    a. Carbonation
    b. Soil characteristics
    c. Age
    d. Grape characteristics

33. Which of the following does *not* refer to a Scotch?
    a. White Label
    b. Black Label
    c. Yellow Label
    d. Red Label

34. Which of the following does not come in a square bottle?
    a. Chambord
    b. Cointreau
    c. Amaretto
    d. Beefeater

35. Which of the following liqueurs is clear?
    a. Peach schnapps
    b. Galliano
    c. Frangelico
    d. Metaxa 5 Star

36. Cocktails that contain tonic water always get which of the following?
    a. Vodka or gin
    b. Highball glass
    c. Lime garnish
    d. Large drinking straw

37. Which of the following liqueurs would most likely be stored on the top shelf?
    a. Louis XIII
    b. Baileys Irish Cream
    c. DeKuyper's peppermint schnapps
    d. Sambuca Romana

38. Which of the following is not a cognac?
    a. Sempe Armagnac
    b. Rémy Martin VSOP
    c. Martell
    d. Hennessy VS

39. Which of the following is not clear?
    a. Absolut citron
    b. Rumple Mintz
    c. Bombay Sapphire
    d. Grand Marnier 150

40. An "in-and-out martini" means:
   a. The bartender stirs it quickly
   b. The customer leaves right after drinking it
   c. Vermouth is dumped out before the gin is added
   d. The olive is dipped in and then removed

Answers: 1-B; 2-D; 3-D; 4-D; 5-C; 6-A; 7-B; 8-C; 9-A;
           10-A; 11-A; 12-C; 13-D; 14-A; 15-B; 16-D; 17-B; 18-A; 19-C; 20-A; 21-B; 22-D; 23-B; 24-C;
           25-D; 26-B; 27-A; 28-C; 29-D; 30-C; 31-A; 32-A; 33-C; 34-A; 35-A; 36-C; 37-A; 38-A; 39-D;
           40-C

Scoring: 35–40 correct. *You're a pro.*
           30–35 correct. *You're an apprentice.*
           25–30 correct. *You're a rookie.*
           Fewer than 25 correct. *You're hopeless. Go into management.*

GLOSSARY OF BARTENDERS' SLANG

aisle
The area in a banquet facility behind the banquet rooms where the staff operates and liquor and supplies are stored.

backbar
The area of shelves behind the bartender on which the bottles are displayed.

badaboom
After you insult a customer, whether accidentally or on purpose, say, ''Badaboom!'' and smile, and that'll get you out of it.

ball and a beer
A highball and a beer, which some people drink at the same time, or a shot of whiskey and a beer.

barfly
A person who spends too much time in bars.

barred
Forbidden to enter a particular drinking establishment because of unacceptable behavior.

barrel
A keg of beer.

beer-and-shot joint
A drinking establishment, usually a corner pub, where foo-foo drinks are not served.

belly up
To stand up to the bar, as in "Hey, Joe, belly up to the bar. Next round's on you."

Big Brother
A spotter, shopper, or spy who pretends to be a customer while secretly evaluating your service and trying to catch you feeding the till.

Black
Johnnie Walker Black Label Scotch.

bleed
To open the tap lines in order to remove the stale beer.

blush
Rosé wine or white zinfandel.

bonus
The money that the bartenders divide up among themselves at the end of the night.

bouncer
A person, typically of large size, employed by a drinking establishment to remove unruly customers.

break down
To clean up and put everything away at the end of a shift.

breakfast club
A group of regular early-morning drinkers.

Buca
Sambuca Romana.

buck
An even one hundred dollars, as in "We made a buck last night."

bucket o' blood
A drinking establishment with a reputation as a place where violence breaks out on a regular basis.

build
To add the ingredients one at a time to the glass in preparing a cocktail.

bump
To overpour slightly, as in "He gave the cocktail a little bump."

call liquor
Liquor of a higher quality and price than well liquor, typically called for by brand name.

camper
A customer who remains seated at the bar for an unusually long time, often right up to and past closing time, as in "We ought to give that camper a can of Sterno and some marshmallows."

card
To ask a customer for identification.

carry
To wait on more than your share of customers in order to pick up another bartender's slack, as in "I've been carrying Phil all night."

cash out
To reconcile the cash register receipts at the end of a shift. Also, the actual money and paperwork, as in "Give the cash-out to the manager so we can get out of here and catch last call next door."

century note
A hundred-dollar bill.

chief financial officer
The customer who gets the check, as in "I have the damage right here. Which one of you is the chief financial officer?"

chits
Tickets used to purchase cocktails at a private club or banquet facility.

chump change
A small amount of money in tips.

contact
The customer who is responsible for the tab in a large party.

crank
To make drinks nonstop for a long period of time.

cuff
A running tab or a free drink, as in "Bartender, this one's on the cuff, okay?"

damage
The check, as in "Yo, bartender, what's the damage over here?"

dead soldiers
Empty beer bottles.

dope slap
A slap delivered crisply and unexpectedly to the back of the head of your co-worker behind the bar when he keeps stepping on your foot.

double
A drink made with twice the alcohol called for in the recipe, as in "Bartender, you'd better make that a double . . . in case I like it." Also, two shifts worked back-to-back.

double sawbuck
A twenty-dollar bill.

drag-pour
To overpour by dumping the contents of the jigger into the cocktail while the liquor is still flowing from the speed pourer.

draw
To pour a tap beer, as in "Bartender, draw me one of them Millers."

drawer
The part of the cash register where the money is kept, as in "Check under the drawer for any large bills."

dupe
The duplicate of the order sheet that members of the wait staff present at the service bar to get a cocktail.

ear bender
A customer who engages a bartender in a lengthy, boring, one-sided conversation with little or no understanding of the fact that the bartender has other customers to wait on.

eighty-six
To announce that a particular item has run out and is no longer available, as in, "Eighty-six the piña colada mix. Yahoo!"

feeding the till
Stealing money by placing cash from a sale in the drawer without ringing it up.

Fire in the hole!
A warning that the bartender is about to dump a bucket of ice into the ice bin at the bar.

five-spot
A five-dollar bill.

flag
A garnish consisting of a cherry pinned to the outside of an orange or pineapple slice with a toothpick or sword pick.

flat out
At maximum speed, as in "We were flat out for four hours."

float
Liquor poured on top of a cocktail, as in "Bartender, float some Myers's on that."

floor
The dining room of a restaurant, as an area separate from the bar, or the wait staff, as in "He didn't have what it takes to be a bartender so they put him to work on the floor."

foo-foo drinks
Frozen cocktails that are time-consuming to make.

free-pour
To pour the alcohol without the aid of a jigger, relying on instinct or experience to determine the proper amount.

gun
A device kept in a holster at the drink station and used to dispense sodas, water, and sometimes liquor.

hair of the dog
Any alcoholic drink taken as a cure for a hangover. In folk medicine, "the hair of the dog that bit you" was believed to prevent infection from a dog bite.

hangover
The aftereffects of heavy alcohol consumption, including headache and nausea.

happy hour
A designated time when cocktails are sold at reduced prices or when appetizers are free.

hatchet man
A bar or restaurant manager who specializes in and enjoys firing workers.

head
The foam on top of a beer or a shaken cocktail.

highball
An old term for a whiskey and ginger ale served in an 8-ounce or 10-ounce cocktail glass. Also refers to the type of glass.

hit
To make another cocktail, as in "Bartender, hit me again, will you?"

house pour
The well liquor or the wine served by the glass in a particular establishment.

igloo
A device placed around a bottle of white wine to keep it cold.

in the weeds
A state of mind that occurs during busy periods when orders back up and problems occur, characterized by a feeling of helplessness and panic.

Jack
Jack Daniel's sour mash whiskey.

jamming
Working at full speed in especially hectic conditions.

jar
Any receptacle behind the bar in which tips are placed.

Jewish milkshake
Four ounces of Glenlivet Scotch in a large tulip glass packed with ice, given its name by the famous Boston bookmaker, Louie Saks.

jigger
A small metal cup, shaped like two cones attached at the points, used to measure liquid poured into a cocktail.

Johnny Jingo
Any particularly annoying customer with a lot of quirks and peculiar habits.

kick
To run out. A keg kicks when it runs out of beer and sends a blast of air and foam out of the tap.

kill
To destroy a dupe, or slip, so that cocktails are not made twice at the service bar.

lace
To pour an ingredient, such as grenadine, in a circular motion on top of a cocktail.

last call
The last chance for customers to order a cocktail before the bar closes at the end of the evening, as in "Hurry up or we're never going to make it over there before last call."

layer
To pour liqueurs in separate layers in the serving glass.

lines
The plastic tubes that carry the beer from the keg room to the taps at the bar, or carry soda from the boxes to the gun.

marry
To combine the liquor from two partially full bottles so that one empty bottle can be discarded.

middle shelf
A category of liquors that is above well liquor but below top shelf. Beefeater gin and Smirnoff vodka are middle-shelf brands.

milking the clock
Remaining punched in on the time clock after your shift is over and your work is done.

mist
A cocktail, such as a Scotch mist, made by pouring straight liquor over crushed ice.

neat
Served straight up and un-chilled, as in "Bartender, give me a Dewar's neat."

nurse
To make a cocktail or beer last for a long, long time, as in "This guy's going to nurse that one beer all night again."

on the rocks
Over ice.

overpour
To put more liquor into the cocktail than called for by the recipe.

perfect manhattan
A manhattan that contains both sweet and dry vermouth.

plastic
Payment by credit card, as in "Bartender, I'm going to put that on plastic tonight."

poco grande
A tulip-shaped glass with a large capacity.

point
The front station of a horseshoe-shaped bar, or the part of any bar that juts out into the crowd, as in "Okay, who's got the point tonight?"

poison
Liquor, as in "Name your poison."

pony
A small stemmed cordial glass that holds one ounce.

pony up
To pay your portion of the check.

pounding
Consuming one drink after another with little time in between. A customer who is pounding might need to be shut off soon.

pouring cost
The percentage of the gross income of the bar associated with the cost of the liquor.

proof
The amount of alcohol in a particular liquor, expressed as twice the actual percentage—86 proof gin, for example, is 43 percent alcohol.

pull
To pour tap beer, as in "Bartender, pull me a Guinness stout."

rail
The narrow shelf at the drink station slightly below the bar surface on which glasses are placed while cocktails are being mixed.

Red
Johnnie Walker Red Label Scotch.

regular
Any customer who comes in on a regular basis.

ring up
To operate the cash register and put money in the till.

Rockefeller
A cheap customer who regularly leaves a below average tip, as in "He's a real Rockefeller, that one."

rocking chair
During a busy shift at a three-man bar, one bartender is the rocking chair when the other two have the entire bar covered.

round
A second set of identical drinks for two or more customers.

rubberneck
To sweep all of one's change off the bar, even the dimes and nickels, as in "Boy, that stiff is really rubberneckin' tonight."

running
Being made to take extra steps, as in "This Johnny Jingo is really running me."

sawbuck
A ten-dollar bill.

service bar
A station with no stools for customers, where drinks are made for the wait staff to carry to customers on the floor.

shift drink
A drink awarded an employee at the completion of a shift.

shooter
A drink served straight up and consumed in one gulp.

short-arm
To avoid picking up the tab as if your arms were too short to reach your pockets, as in "Don't short-arm me on this one. It's your turn."

shot
A one- to two-ounce serving of a single liquor or liqueur.

shut off
To refuse to serve any more alcohol to a customer.

skip
To walk out without paying one's tab.

slammed
Rushed, or suddenly crowded. The bar is slammed when a large number of customers arrive at the same time.

sleeve
A container, usually made of marble, that is chilled in a cooler and used to keep a wine bottle cold at the bar or at a table.

slip
The dupe, or duplicate copy, of the drink order that the service bartender receives, as in "Guys, kill your slips, or I'll be making these drinks twice and our pouring cost will go up."

snifter
A balloon-shaped glass used primarily for brandy.

soda back
A glass of soda water, with or without ice, served along with another drink, usually straight liquor, as in "Bartender, give me a Glenlivet up, soda back."

speed pourer
A metal or plastic spout that fits into the neck of a liquor bottle, enabling the bartender to control the flow of the liquor even when the bottle is turned upside down.

speed rack
The metal rack near the bartender's knees in which all the well liquor is kept for easy access.

spike
To destroy a dupe, or slip, so a cocktail won't be made twice at the service bar. Also, to add extra liquor.

splash
A half-second push of the button on the soda or water gun, or a small amount of any liquid added to a cocktail.

spotter
Big Brother—spy hired by management to watch the bartenders to evaluate their service and see if they are overpouring or feeding the till.

spotter's report
The written evaluation turned in to management by Big Brother.

station
The area where drinks are made or customers are served at the bar.

stiff
To leave no tip. Also, a customer who doesn't tip.

straight up
Served with no ice, but sometimes chilled over ice and then strained.

suds
Beer, as in "Hey, bartender, gimme another glass of suds."

tap
The spigot through which keg beer is dispensed. Also, the act of connecting a keg to the lines.

three deep
Very busy, with throngs of customers crowding up against the bar, as in "The bar was three deep all night and we were really in the weeds for a while, but at least we made a buck and a half each."

tighten
To serve another cocktail or another round, as in "Hey, bartender, tighten me up over here, will you?"

till
The cash register or the cash register drawer.

tin roof special
A free drink.

top shelf
The most expensive and finest quality liquors and liqueurs, typically displayed on the top shelf of the backbar.

tower
The insulated unit to which the beer taps are attached at the bar.

tulip glass
A stemmed glass with a large capacity typically used for frozen cocktails.

up-selling
Persuading a customer to order a higher shelf, thus more expensive, liquor instead of well liquor.

walkout
A tab that is left unpaid because the customer skipped.

war debt
A large check or tab presented to a customer.

water back
A glass of ice water served along with another drink, usually straight liquor, as in "Bartender, give me a Jack straight, water back."

well
The speed rack of liquor bottles near the bartender's knees at the drink station.

well liquor
The liquor kept in the speed rack, typically the cheapest that money can buy.

White Label
Dewar's Scotch, as in "Bartender, give me a double White Label on the rocks, splash of soda, twist, water back."